the INDIANOLA REVIEW

WINTER 2015

Cover Price: $11.00

the INDIANOLA REVIEW

ISSUE ONE • WINTER 2015

EDITOR
Danny Judge

MANAGING EDITOR
Amy Brady

ASSOCIATE EDITOR
Hannah Bassett

FICTION EDITOR
Anne Weisgerber

POETRY EDITOR
Anthony Frame

NONFICTION EDITOR
A. A. Weiss

CONTRIBUTING EDITORS
Karen Hopper
Erin Kaempf

READERS

Chelsie Abney
Lori Sambol Brody
Geosi Gyasi
Zachary Kocanda
John Lee MacDonald
Jennifer Met
Kirsten Miles

Gabe Montesanti
Erica Mosley
Rachel Van Sickle
Jan Elman Stout
Joseph Walters
Audrey Webb
Natalie Wilson

Subscriptions: $35.00 for one year (4 Issues); Published quarterly: March, June, September, December; Single issues: $11.00.

Submissions: We read year round and charge no reading fee for standard submissions. Read our guidelines carefully before submitting. To subscribe or submit, visit us at indianolareview.com.

The Indianola Review
Issue One | Published December 2015
ISBN: 978-0692592328

Indianola Press

© 2015 The Indianola Review
IndianolaReview.com

Cover: *The Enigma,* by Gustave Doré, 1871

FICTION

POETRY

NONFICTION

MISCELLANEOUS

OTHER INTERESTING THINGS

The Place You're Supposed to Laugh

This was the place she was supposed to laugh. She was a half-beat late; those familiar with the rhythms of Scot's stories had already turned toward her. It was important that she laugh now. If she didn't laugh—if she waited even a moment longer—it would mean that Scot was cruel. And surely he was not cruel—not Scot, charming Scot, witty Scot, surgically observant Scot who would not notice your new haircut, per se, but the uncanny resemblance you now bore to your mother.

In the story Scot was telling, Irene was in the Health/Self-Help section of the Barnes & Noble, looking vainly and with mounting desperation for tonight's book, *Love Medicine.* When the clerk arrived to offer assistance, Irene explained that what she was looking for was a romantic advice book. Having misread a book group email, Irene had been under the impression that the author of *Love Medicine* was a Native American mystic who had written down well-guarded tribal secrets to a rewarding, lasting marriage.

This had all been re-created by Scot as a sort of apology for the fact that neither of them had read *Love Medicine* for tonight. He had performed a wicked impersonation of Irene's confusion in the bookstore, raising the pitch of his voice to a tremulous whine. But what he said was true: she had called ahead, spoken to someone named Brad, who assured her that the store did in fact have *three* copies of *Love Medicine* on hand; she had repeated these facts to the bookstore clerk. The accuracy of what Scot said did not make his words hurt less.

Perhaps, Scot said in Irene's voice, I ought to be dealing with *Brad.*

This line elicited his biggest laugh yet. It would have been a very good time for Irene to join in. Instead, she sipped from her wine glass.

"So, honey," Scot said, "just so you know. The book for next month? *Mistress of Spices?* It's not a cookbook, sweetie."

Ba-*dum*-dum.

The other wives were waiting, silent, for her signal. Clear her throat, move away from Scot toward their cluster near the windows, and they would know: Scot had gone too far. They and their husbands would be pleasant enough for the remainder of the evening, of course, but they would know, and they would tell each other later that they'd always known. That she was a saint for putting up with him so long.

Mercifully, she laughed. Her laugh was perhaps too loud and too long, but she was compensating for its lateness. The women were grateful to her for it. Irene described her embarrassment when the clerk in Goth makeup explained that Louise Erdrich was a novelist, and that her books, all eight of them, were shelved in the fiction section. *She's kinda famous,* the clerk had said. Irene radiated warmth—even her professed shame was lovely—at the group, though perhaps not exactly at Scot.

Honestly, Irene didn't know what had happened with this month's book. She was saying something now about the weather, how this summer had just been a little off. A woman in purple assured Irene that she understood. Her name was Sharon, and she wasn't sure Irene had missed much, as she hadn't liked *Love Medicine* as much as that one about the family in Baltimore. Irene said again that she couldn't believe the heat this summer.

When she'd first joined the book group, Irene had not anticipated the importance of the right food, the right wine. She and Scot could afford it, but still, it caused her stress to stand before the store's enormous selection and try to choose not just a good one—anyone could go with the Sinskey Pinot Noir—but a surprising one, a fresh choice to which someone would say, Irene, wherever did you find this?

Several of the women recognized the chutney-filled mushroom caps from last month's *Gourmet*; Irene had done an uncanny job replicating the layout, even placing them on a silver tray similar to that in the magazine and drizzling the edges with a pale pink sauce. Like the house, like Irene herself, like the apricot-colored blouse and flowy black slacks she was wearing, the mushrooms were impeccable.

It was particularly important to have the right wine, the right cheese, the right ceviche in small lotus-root cups on the night she had not read—had not even managed to locate without assistance from a vampiric teenager—the assigned book. But *Love Medicine* had been a departure for the group. Several recent choices had been memoirs by women and men not unlike Irene and Scot, couples who'd relocated to some western European country, bought a rambling, run-down villa/chateau/*weingut*, and proceeded to immerse themselves in its restoration, leading to many humorous encounters with local craftsmen (*Mais monsieur, nous ont avons le système métrique!*), eccentric innkeepers and grocers, and the consequent enrichment of lives and loves. Although one or two group members had complained about the repetitive themes of these memoirs, Irene had been rather taken with them. She had begun to keep in her writing desk a list of countries which had not yet been covered in this vein: Greece, Ireland, Portugal. The recent publication of Isadore Tucker's *Promises of Prague* had caused her to draw a line through Czechoslovakia. Although Scot maintained that such a trip would hardly be conducive to his career, Irene felt sure that he, like the workaholic husband of the author of *Conjugating Être*, would be won over by the sun, the quirky locals, and the pleasures of a well-sanded oak floor.

Irene did not want pity from her book group. It would be a little obscene, considering her comfort, her husband's inordinate wealth that had somehow lasted when their own portfolios had shriveled and turned white like limes abandoned in the fruit drawer after the gin's run out. It would not be proper for one of *them* to presume to comfort *her*. Even after a summer like this one.

In May, the police had begun putting signs on the freeways to help find abducted children. They were the sort of signs used to warn of a closed exit ramp or high winds. But starting in May the lights spelled out WHITE HONDA with a license plate number, or BLUE FORD ESCORT. Irene found herself staring into the backseats of sedans, looking for pigtailed girls with red-rimmed eyes or kids who looked lost in the shocking, sudden absence of a car seat and sing-along tape.

The media had been unable to decide whether the rash of child abductions was a real phenomenon or whether it only felt like an epidemic to a nation so recently wounded. A previously unsuspecting public was now alert to omnipresent danger: anyone anywhere might wish to do one harm. There was Melissa Diaz, from Fremont, whose friends had made a giant poster saying WE MISS YOU, MISSY, whose mother crossed herself on Channel 4 and begged for her angel's return, whose best friend still wore her half of a locket, sure that Missy would be found and would once again press her half into place to complete the silver heart. Missy had reportedly been spotted in a red Maxima, and Irene sought her out in traffic. She peered at the tinted back windows of vans. She was prepared to swerve her car in front of the one holding Missy Diaz, to give her own life up for Missy's safe recovery.

Next to her, Sharon was smoothing the front of her purple dress and keeping up the book group badinage. "We're still getting settled in the new house," she said. "I know it's not that far away, but it feels as if we've entered a parallel universe."

Irene told her that she wouldn't believe Marin was as bad as people said. After all, she used to believe the worst about California, and now she couldn't believe she'd ever lived anywhere else.

"They've got a thing now," Sharon said, "where the migrant workers, or immigrants anyway, wait on the freeway on-ramps, and people pick them up for their commutes, just so they can use the carpool lane. I think the workers take the bus back, afterward."

The wives near the windows shook their heads sadly, as if to say that although this struck them as outrageous and deplorable, they weren't surprised to hear it. It was postulated that the practice had been imported from Southern California, from Orange County.

"But," Irene said in a crystalline voice, "what do they talk about?"

Scot overheard this and joined the circle to begin a stand-up routine about the morning conversation between a wealthy Walnut Creek matron and a heavily accented worker who said mostly: "okeydokey" and "Si, señora." The group yielded a modest snicker when he came to the part about them going through a Starbucks drive-thru. He rolled the "r" in Frappuccino extravagantly. Scot's laugh was now the loudest in the room. He finished up with a short exchange between the same two people, now on their way home: "And how was your day, Juan?" "Okeydokey." "Same time tomorrow?" "Si, señora."

Irene performed an elaborate pantomime of a hostess who has just realized her guests' glasses are empty and went for the wine in the kitchen. If she didn't know better she would think that Scot had been working on that carpooling monologue for weeks. It was worse than that, though; he could now begin one of his riffs out of nowhere, on the wispiest premise: a mispronounced word or a shampoo ad she'd found unexpectedly moving, and he was off. This, of course, was the cleverness for which her husband was celebrated. That he could be so clever, so in tune with both technology's capabilities and the market's vagaries and at the same time retain a youthful sensibility, described in one industry magazine as a "startlingly unforced whimsy," was something of a marvel. The magazines were titillated by his habit of spending his company's outsize profits in frivolous ways. "Boy wonder," they called Scot, and "young-at-heart mogul." He wore hoodies and ironic T-shirts, as if to disguise his ambition and corporate bloodlust. Spent whole afternoons playing video games with the kid who lived next door. And in the kitchen Scot had scattered half the alphabet, in primary-colored magnets, on the side of the Sub-Zero.

When Irene returned, she bypassed the group Scot had hijacked. Instead, she joined two husbands who were looking over her CDs. She could hear Scot telling stories about the movie filming in front of his office, the starlet who yesterday emerged thirty-seven times from a black convertible with a camera that began at her feet panning slowly up each time. *Thirty-seven times,* said Scot again.

This was not fair; one's husband should not share so overtly his delight in another woman's legs. Especially when his wife was as striking as Irene. But as the group could not be sure whether she'd heard him, they laughed guiltily with Scot.

One of the husbands had pulled out the CD soundtrack of *Cats.* His daughter's second grade class had just performed an edited version, he said. Irene said she wished she'd seen it. This was an absurd thing for her to say—imagine, Scot MacAvoy's wife showing up to watch eight-year-olds gyrate to "Rum Tum Tugger." Later, on the drive home, he and his wife would debrief: Irene seemed a bit off, and it wasn't just that she hadn't read the book. But, he would add, that would've been nice.

She was not sure how long this would last, this business of blaming the summer, the heat. It was already September—well into the new school year. She'd seen the children gathered on the playground outside the elementary school near her house. Last year she and Scot made a donation for new playground equipment: recycled wood swings from old car tires and soft sand instead of gravel at the foot of the slide. The school planned to put a plaque near the rope ladder with their names, but Irene asked them not to. She did not want the children who climbed the rope ladder and the ecofriendly "rock" wall to learn her name this way.

She had her favorites: the red-haired girl in tall socks and a short skirt, pale knees just showing as she swung herself across the bars; the boy with glasses who clambered up the rock wall with balletic grace.

She would have preferred to be known to them as Nathaniel's mother. Nathaniel would have joined them on the playground, would have played shortstop in their kickball games and would have had, she suspected, a bit of a crush on the red-haired girl. She believed the children would have liked him, though she considered the possibility that he would have been too clever to be popular, a bit too much of his father in him.

Of course, if he had wanted to play third base, or outfield, well that would have been just fine.

Sharon and Jim were leaving. Irene helped Sharon get her wrap around her shoulders.

At last, the breeze from the water was back, bringing an end to the stifling Indian summer. Irene had had enough of the heat, enough remembering the weight of Nathaniel, growing, pulling her spine into a curve. Too many children had been stolen.

"Well, goodnight, Irene," said Sharon's husband. Then, as if it had just occurred to him, as if he had never done this before, he sang a bit of "Goodnight, Irene." His singing voice was slightly sharp. Sharon wore a beatific smile. Irene patted the man's hand, said goodnight and leaned against the door after she'd closed it.

Perhaps, she thought, she had been greedy, with a husband who was an everlasting twelve-year-old Boy Wonder, to wish for a son. Perhaps she was not owed Nathaniel; perhaps she had not deserved him.

Last Thursday she decided to surprise Scot with a picnic lunch at work. This was something they used to do, in the early days, when the company was only Scot and his friend Mike; even Irene herself made phone calls and designed the logo. Before either a foosball or a conference table had appeared. Mike had rented a space for them in a former tanning salon; the scent of cocoa butter had seeped into the carpet and lingered. Their workdays were enlivened by periodic discoveries: a forgotten cache of the metallic swim goggles worn by tanners or an abandoned ultraviolet bulb. Scot would carry it into the room like a king's scepter, proclaiming a new treasure from the erstwhile Bronze Age. Irene would bring sandwiches, and the three of them would spread a towel over the carpet in the reception area to eat.

On Thursday she had picked up the sandwiches at Draeger's: salmon with red peppers for herself, roasted eggplant for Scot. Mike, of course, had long vanished from the boardroom, having allowed Scot to buy out his share in the mid-nineties. The edging out of Mike had been gradual but decisive: Scot's ruthlessness was so charming and casual it seemed almost accidental. For her picnic, Irene took along a half-size bottle of Bordeaux, because this was the sort of thing the CEO's wife could do, because she too was capable of unforced whimsy, and she packed it all into the wicker hamper, for old time's sake. And she'd come to the block on which Scot's office stood when a man in a Dodgers hat stopped her.

"Sorry, ma'am," he said, "the set is closed."

"The set?" Irene said, but then she saw that the block was slick with simulated rain and that a dozen extras were sprinkled about with umbrellas and shopping bags. A pair of women pointed into the front window of Scot's offices as if they'd discovered a must-have pair of shoes. Another woman pushed a baby carriage Irene recognized as an expensive British brand she had ordered for Nathaniel. Scot had warned her not to order things so early, but she was too excited to wait. But the thing about rules like the three-month waiting period is that when you haven't told your friends you're pregnant, it's tricky to tell them that you're not anymore.

"Cue rain," the man shouted.

And she stood there, with her basket of gourmet food disguised as a homemade picnic, outside the company run by a man pretending to be a carefree twelve-year-old, herself the very image of a well-provided-for woman *not* prone to crying jags on behalf of abducted Latino children or standing mournfully outside elementary school playgrounds; she stood there transfixed by a patently false cloudburst.

Even the not-truth hurt.

They would find her, Missy Diaz, in a ravine somewhere. By the time they knew who took her, it would be something else: the economy, war, screenwriters on strike, or all three. When Irene read the follow-up Missy Diaz stories—they would be small, in the back of the California section—she would remember the movie set, the localized artificial rain shower, the picnic basket she'd left in front of a lady with a sign that said SICK WOMAN TRYING REAL HARD, a woman who did not know the rain was manufactured, did not realize that if she'd walked a hundred yards she would have been safely back in Silicon Valley, where it was seventy-five and sunny.

The Mosquito, the Bird, and the Honeybee

We have flown through
the wood, tiny slats

of darkness hovering near
the incandescence of wings,

the pop and buzz of the short
stop, the earth pop,

the bigger canvas stretched
to the end of the cobblestones,

and we are the end of waiting,
the inner light of things,

hard and pushing questions
where they go, corners

and rounded off middles
and bubble bath Sundays

with family and start
and middle and art

and finished with chevron
and tired of knick knacks,

and oh, silly boy, this space
is where I leave you.

Stacey Balkun

The domestic mermaid went to the art museum

to see an exhibit of women surrealists.

She was especially taken with Dorothea Tanning
and her "Arizona Landscape" because she knew
how the artist felt—she herself was trapped

in Fresno, but dreamed of sea—
hardpan growing out of her skull, waterfalls

somewhere in the nearby mountains
but always just over shoulder,
just too far away

to see.
A crown of crepe myrtle and tupelo

instead of hairs, dead cells hanging from a scalp
as tangled as grape vines
that smell of spending too long in the tub

of bathwater, stagnant as an old tide pool,
her body limp as dead crabs or wilted seaweed.

Open Letter to Museum Director in Charge
of Brain Placement

Dear Madam/Sir,

Please forgive me if I offend with this open letter, but I am not exactly sure to whom I should address my concerns, as I am but a plastic model of the brain of *Tupaia belangeri*, Northern Treeshrew.

Since my transfer from off-site storage in the spring, I have truly enjoyed my tenure on display. Words cannot express how honored I feel to be part of the magnificent assemblage of brains with which you have seen fit to place me.

Keeping my admiration of your work in mind, then, please understand that the intent of this letter is not to provoke, but merely to inform you of certain areas of concern within the specimens under your purview. As a humble recent addition to your distinguished cadre of organs, I feel I owe you no less than the opportunity to learn of these conditions so that you may address them according to your own wishes.

To provide you as much assistance as possible, I have taken the liberty of proposing solutions for each item below. After all, as my wise little mother used to tell me, "Problems without proposals are merely complaints."

1) Disposition: by which I primarily refer to object placement within the exhibit. However, as I need not explain to a museum director, specimen placement does affect specimen temperament, and so the term means, for our purposes, one and the same.

I have been placed in the Animal Anatomy Exploration Center, Quadrant 1b of the middle shelf of Vitrine A. I remind you of my placement close to the entrance not to insinuate your ignorance, but to situate, as it were, my concern: The first thing hundreds of visitors see as they stream into the Center is me, roughly the size of a cherry pit, on the same shelf as the watermelon-sized brain of a whale. While this juxtaposition masterfully demonstrates the diversity in brain development throughout the animal kingdom, I regret to inform you it does so at the expense of my self-esteem.

Imagine spending your day constantly hearing remarks about how small, how tiny, how insignificant you are. This has become my existence. The whale brain, meanwhile, grumbles at being wasted in a sham competition, its majesty squandered like that of the magnificent lion in a clown act.

Meanwhile in Vitrine B, the squirrel, chipmunk, and African mouse brains cower in a constant state of anxiety on the same shelf as the coyote brain. Loath as I would be to join the coyote brain, I feel I would be a more appropriate companion for a society of small mammals than for a leviathan of the ocean.

Thus I propose a switch between myself with the coyote brain, to allow similar species to congregate, while simultaneously giving the whale brain a slightly worthier object of comparison. I have polled all brains potentially affected by the move (except, of course, the coyote brain), and they would all be in favor.

2) I have noticed a general sense of malaise among the plastic specimens in Vitrines A, B, and C. Perhaps this is intentional; perhaps I have not been with the company long enough to understand its *esprit de corps*. I have attempted, but have ultimately failed, to glean some sense of sophistication from their world-weary approach. And somehow I am not convinced that "dusty, muddled, and sad" was your intended vision for this exhibit.

I therefore propose a regular cleaning regimen for the objects and canisters (more on this later) of the exhibit. Sprucing up the vitrines would certainly improve morale—remove some of the dust from old souls, as it were. I understand that this would require certain arrangements to improve access to the specimens without leaving them vulnerable to the curious fingers of children. I have been made aware of last year's turkey brain choking scare, and I shudder to fathom the depths to which I myself might have sunk.

May I also recommend retouching the sad, waxy pallor of some of the more senior plastic pieces? The poor old dears, some of them chipped, cling to mere memories of vibrant red and blue blood vessels coursing over their formerly pinkish folds and crevices. The mere flick of a paintbrush could bring these elders closer to their former glory, thereby boosting the whole community.

3) I include this last point at the risk of sounding exclusionary, perhaps even bigoted, which I most certainly am not. But I must be plain: I am still struggling to understand the placement of a handful of organic specimens in jars of fluid next to plastic specimens such as myself. Because I am new, I have attempted to learn the advantages of this juxtaposition by discussing it with others; through these discussions I have found that I am not alone in my questioning of it. The scarcity of organic specimens imbues them with a sense of celebrity/specialness that has a negative effect on the psyche of common plastic models like myself. It is, simply put, bad for morale.

The only solution I have been able to devise involves moving the jars holding organic specimens out of the Vitrine A-C vicinity entirely. I realize that this is a drastic and distasteful tactic and would therefore welcome an opportunity to discuss alternative solutions with you.

If this letter reaches you, Madame/Mister Museum Director, I would like to thank you in advance for considering my concerns. I am completely aware that all decisions on which issues to tackle and by what means are completely under your control. I stand ready, should you choose, to advise you in any way possible on the situations listed above. You can reach me in Vitrine A, middle shelf, Quadrant 1b.

Respectfully,

Plastic Brain, *Tupaia belangeri* (Northern Treeshrew)

Carrie Meadows

God Sent the Gun:
My grandfather explains why he did it

The gun says, You don't have to take that, you
earned the money in your pocket losing
half a finger like your daddy's left leg
to the cutter. The gun says, Your daddy
thumped his love hard into your head—what more
do your boys need than to feel their scalps sting?
Your girl will fair fine. She has her mamma's eyes.
The gun says, Turn your check to booze though
you want cheekbones high and blushed, your wife's
before she held your babies and not you
through the night. The gun says, Four Roses
will do until you come home and she turns
your pockets inside out but won't look at you.
I never knew my fists could become bombs.

I never knew my fists could become bombs
busting flesh and plaster. The gun whispers,
Keep me in the dresser for nights your knees
lock, and, hammer cocked, you start to believe
in the end of punchcards, in the cheekbones
you'd want to kiss if only you could find
your way back to that whippoorwill night
she held your chin and fed you pecan pie.
The gun says, The bar is open for you.
Go to the back room where you can fade
into the silver ball skating its maze
of red, blue and yellow lights shouting bell
and storm as you slip quietly between
the flippers like rain dodging wiper blades.

Arrow in Translation

I don't speak another language
or have anything to tell you
in any tongue not my own,
I'm not on a small road
in a foreign country,
in a wood I don't recognize
the glossolalia of what,
a thousand birds betrayed
by their song strangled
in a thicket,
and yet I'm often traveling,
pulled by the roots,
caught in a flutter,
or as I was about to say,
quivering.

James Reed

Simpatico

My parents are cruel to my brother.
So he says.
I've no reason to doubt him.
Join the club, I'd say, if I wanted a word in edgewise.

When All the Stars Are Dead

We were almost ready to close when these two Buddhist monks walked in and ordered twenty large cheese pizzas to go.

"Sorry, we lock up in five minutes," I said. "We've got a few leftover slices but—"

Kelly stood behind the register with a sour grimace, strangling a knotted dishtowel with pink-tipped hands.

"We're closed," she said, staring at the counter, hiding her eyes. "There's a twenty-four-hour Pizza Hut a mile down the road."

"Yes, we know," the shorter of the two monks said. "But Brother Phap Dong prefers *your* pizza. It's his last meal. Tomorrow, at sunrise, he's setting himself on fire. You'll help us, yes? Phap Dong has a beautiful heart."

The monks smiled, mystical and serene, practically oozing loving-kindness from their big, shaved heads. They wore dark-maroon robes and plain brown sandals; the shorter one was Asian, Vietnamese, I think; the other monk was a Jersey guy like me. I wasn't certain, but he resembled some guy my older brother used to beat up in high school.

"Wait a minute—he's setting himself on fire?"

"Yes, for the benefit of all sentient beings."

"He asked specifically for *your* pizza," Jersey Monk said. "Phap Dong says he knows you. Sometimes you visit the sangha."

Kelly looked at me and scowled, as if she'd just seen my naked picture and was disappointed by the reveal. There was a monastery ten miles outside town, and I sometimes stopped and listened to the talks. I wasn't a Buddhist, but much of what I heard made sense, and I had started reading books by the Dalai Lama. I was trying to develop my mind, avoid being the lunkhead behind the pizza counter I seemed fated to become. In college I had studied literature and philosophy for two semesters before dropping out, too broke to afford tuition, too nervous for the ball-and-chain of a student loan. I knew a little something about debt. During my senior year in high school, my father went bankrupt and put a bullet in his brain.

Kelly could tell I was wavering. The monks didn't say anything, but they didn't leave, either. They folded their hands in a prayer position and waited. From my visits to the monastery I knew they could stay that way forever, that they lived in the *now*.

"It's going to take at least an hour, maybe longer," I said. Before Kelly could throw her hissy fit, I told her to go home. She wouldn't have been much help anyway; her job was handling the register—she'd never made a pizza in her life. I flipped the oven switches and pulled some dough from the fridge.

"Thank you, Flynn," Asian Monk said.

I was shocked he knew my name.

"You're part of the sangha, giving yourself to help others, to help brother Phap Dong. Your heart, too, is beautiful."

Kelly snorted and rolled her eyes, grabbing her purse from under the counter, shooting me a *sucker!* look as she blew past the monks and hustled out the door.

"So what's the deal with twenty pizzas this time of night?" I asked.

"We're down on the Green," Jersey Monk said. "Phap Dong wants to share his last meal."

For the past two weeks, about fifty activists had set up camp on the Green at the center of town—mostly college kids but a few unemployed corporate types, too, along with some hippie grandmothers and a few wandering stoners. My wife, Kasey, and I meant to check it out but hadn't found the time.

"We lead mindfulness sessions on the importance of a peaceful heart," Asian Monk said.

"Even with Right Intention, it's easy to fall into delusion."

"Isn't setting yourself on fire kind of delusional, too?"

"There is controversy, yes, but there is also a tradition of self-immolation among Buddhists. In the Lotus Sutra, it speaks to cultivating the perfection of generosity, the giving of inner wealth. The offering of the body can be a powerful step on the bodhisattva path."

Jersey Monk walked toward the soda case, his face twisted and grim. I could tell he disagreed, but he didn't want to say it. In New

Jersey we only set fires when insurance money was involved. He grabbed a Coke, pulled the cap, and drained half the can.

"In many ways we're all on a course of self-immolation," Asian Monk said. "There's so much greed and violence and delusion. We're burning the planet that sustains us. Is filling your car with gasoline any different from what brother Phap Dong is doing?"

"It hurts a lot less."

Jersey Monk snorted, hiding his face behind the soda can. I started kneading the dough, rolling it out and working it through my fingers, stretching it thin and pressing it back into a ball. It was all muscle memory, my hands like ghosts, squeezing and rolling.

I slid the first batch of pies into the oven and checked my phone: three new messages from Kasey, each one a photograph of a potential tattoo: a flower, a fish, a baby bird hatching from its shell—all finalists for the open real estate on the back of her right calf. Kasey was a cardiac tech at County Hospital; during her downtime she'd send photographs of different designs, mostly for herself but some for me, too. So far, I'd avoided getting inked. Kasey had all kinds of ideas for what we could do with my skin, but I was hesitant, reluctant to traffic in permanent marks.

I texted her back about the last one, the baby bird breaking from its shell: "idk either."

A month earlier we had discovered she was pregnant. It was totally unplanned, unexpected, and in the morning we had an appointment at the clinic to terminate the pregnancy. We were both pro-choice and had serious doubts about bringing a child into this mean, fucked-up world, but as the appointment approached, Kasey had grown sullen and irritable; her Catholic upbringing was hard to shake.

The monks drifted toward the corner, their heads bowed in contemplation as they slipped inside a booth. Their equanimity was unnerving. I knew Phap Dong; he was my age, maybe a few years older, a French Canadian who'd dropped out of college and bummed his way to Asia, looking to screw Thai chicks on the beach and get stoned every night. Instead, he wound up a Buddhist monk.

He liked to play basketball, had a pretty good hook shot. One night at the monastery, we played some hoops in the parking lot, and though he was barefoot and wearing that goofy robe, he still beat me, draining four jumpers at the end to edge me by a point. He had this wild, beautiful laugh, a real graceful soul; he'd elbow you out of his way to grab a rebound but somehow do it mindfully, as if his rebound was *your* rebound, too. I'd never met someone who seemed so at peace with the world. Why would a guy like that self-immolate? My father's suicide: *that* I could understand, even though at the time I hadn't seen it coming.

I was only eighteen, I told myself, as if that mattered.

After the game, as we walked back to the meditation hall, Phap Dong reached into his pocket and handed me a slip of paper. Before I could read it, he placed his hand over mine and whispered: "Later."

It was almost dark, the lights from the parking lot fading as we walked the tree-lined path toward the hall, Phap Dong holding my hand gently, the warmth of his palm spreading across my fingers, both of us silent, the crickets the only sound as we moved down the path. The instinct to pull away was strong and embarrassing, the lunkhead in me screaming, *Push him away before he kisses you.* I'd never held hands with another man, not even my father. When I was too young to cross the street alone, Dad would place his hand on top of my head to guide me, as if he were steering a hand truck. Phap Dong held my hand as if it were the *only* way to walk beside another person.

Later, I opened the slip of paper as I lay in bed. It was a poem: "Buddha in Glory," by Rainer Maria Rilke. Kasey was asleep beside me, still wearing her scrub shirt from the hospital, her bare legs pulled up in a fetal position, an open bottle of Xanax on the nightstand.

I read the poem three times, certain phrases holding my eyes as I scanned the page:

> *Thick fluids rise and flow . . . your flesh, your fruit*
> *A billion stars go spinning through the night.*
> *Now you feel how nothing clings to you;*
> *Your vast shell reaches into endless space.*

To Phap Dong, those words must have felt liberating, but to me endless space seemed terrifying. I *wanted* something to cling to me.

As I settled in beside Kasey, my arm draped over her shoulder, legs tucked against her hips, I kept thinking about the poem, especially the last two lines.

The next morning I stood in the shower, slowly waking, the hot water streaming over my face as I heard the bathroom door creak open and felt a rush of cool air, the curtain sliding back as Kasey joined me. Later that month, when she missed her period, I thought only of that morning, the two of us making love beneath the spray: *thick fluids rise and flow, your flesh, your fruit, your vast shell reaching into endless space.*

When I asked Phap Dong about the poem, he was vague but I kept pushing him. Finally he said, "Perhaps what you see as fixed, is fluid instead."

I thought about my father. I'd found him in our driveway, his body slumped over the steering wheel of our Honda, the windshield speckled red, a wasp perched on the dashboard as if guarding its kill. What could be more fixed than that?

"The next time you sit in meditation," Phap Dong said, "focus on the vast, endless space."

The pizzas were still baking, so I walked over to the monks, hoping they might explain self-immolation.

"Why not ask Phap Dong yourself?" Jersey Monk said. "Come see the encampment. It's important to stand with those who oppose violence and delusion, if for no other reason than your soul demands it."

"Many years ago, my parents were killed by your country's bombs," Asian Monk said. "We lived in Quy Nhon, by the beach. My father was a fisherman, a Buddhist, a peaceful man. My sister and I were visiting our grandmother in another village, or we would have died, too. Why does a country send planes seven thousand miles to kill a poor fisherman and his wife? What kind of delusion causes this to happen? Whenever hatred threatens to consume me, I think of the thousands of your countrymen who went into the streets, who said, 'We must stop.'"

He rose from the booth and walked toward the door, head bowed as he stared through the glass into the dark parking lot. Behind the counter I grabbed the wooden peel and slid a pie from the top oven, cheese bubbling up in blisters of mozzarella and marinara, the crust a rim of golden brown.

Jersey Monk peered over my shoulder as I slid the pie back in the oven and lowered the heat.

"Really, you should come with us," he said. "We walked here, you know. We were hopeful you would drive us back."

"You're out of luck. Our delivery guy left an hour ago and my wife has the car. She won't be here for at least thirty minutes."

"Perfect. She'll come with us, and you can talk with Phap Dong." He set his hand on my shoulder. "He asked for pizza, but he asked for you, too. He wants to speak with you before he leaves us. He said you were in crisis."

"How does he know? I've talked to the guy maybe five or six times."

"Some of the brothers . . . they have a way about them. The third time I visited the sangha, Phap Dien," he nodded toward the Asian Monk, "walked up to me and hugged me before I said a word. He vowed my hurt was his hurt, too, and together we would walk with the pain. They just *know.*"

He grabbed a napkin, wiped his lips, and walked toward the booths.

"Let's sit for a while, the three of us," he said. Phap Dien turned from the door and joined him in the middle of the floor, the two monks folding their legs into the lotus position, robes bunched around their feet as they straightened their posture, closing their eyes.

I wanted to join them, but I was too much in the grip of what Phap Dong called *monkey mind*, my thoughts racing around, helter-skelter, breaking everything in their path. Kasey's pregnancy had thrown us, a challenge to our vow to remain childless. There was too much crap in the world, and, over the years, plenty of it had smacked head-on against our lives. Our relationship was founded on scar tissue. Kasey's stepfather had abused her; there were addiction issues, depression; she'd been a cutter back in high school. Even before my father's suicide, my family was a wreck. My mother left when I was twelve; my older brother later joined the Marines without even saying good-bye. I hadn't heard from either of them in years. My father lost his business, lost our house; he put a gun against his head and fired. It didn't help that Kasey and I were broke, too, her salary gobbled up by student loans, my own paycheck a lousy fourteen bucks an hour, even though I'd been running the place for three years. Bring a child into the world? No thank you; yet I still regretted that we'd never see our baby's face looking up at us with love.

I began boxing up the pizzas, pulling each pie from the oven and sliding it into the box, aware of the monks' steady inhalations, my movements instinctively synched to the rise and fall of their breath. In my pocket was the poem Phap Dong had slipped me at the monastery. I took it out and read it, though I had it memorized. *Now you feel how nothing clings to you; your vast shell reaches into endless space.* Was it mocking me? How did endless space reconcile with my life of constraints, twelve hours-a-day behind the pizza counter, a too-small apartment in a tired suburb, a marriage steeped in a shared sense of doom? Phap Dong had wanted to show me possibilities, but where were they?

I closed the lids on all twenty pizza boxes and packed them in the delivery bags, five boxes per bag, the Velcro straps sealing the heat while we waited for Kasey. I grabbed some napkins and paper plates and threw them in a bag, the scent of all that pizza surrounding me as the monks opened their eyes, raised their heads, and turned to me with peaceful smiles.

The monks sat in the back of the Honda, the pizzas stacked between them as I drove to the Green.

"During break I went down to the maternity ward," Kasey said, staring out the window at the darkened houses lining the road, her weary reflection filling the glass. "There were twelve new mothers. According to the statistics, at least five of the newborns were unplanned. Two mothers will experience some form of postpartum depression, and one will regret her decision to have children. The Pew foundation did a study." She turned from the window. "I thought you might appreciate the data."

"We can always cancel if you're not ready. The doctor said—"

"I know what the doctor said. Just let me feel bitter, okay? We're not canceling."

I found a parking spot a block from the Green and shut the engine. Kasey zipped up her jacket and yawned.

"If you're too tired you can wait in the car," I said, but already she'd unhooked her seat belt and opened the door.

"Let's take a few selfies to prove we were here."

The monks and I split the pizzas and Kasey grabbed the bag of napkins and paper plates as we headed toward the encampment. I was curious, and excited, too, turned on by the possibility of revolution, even a revolution doomed to disperse once the overnight temperatures dropped below forty. Imagining a different way to organize the world seemed important and necessary, and though I was too much of a grinder to ever join them, I was grateful they were out there.

Phap Dien walked beside me as Kasey hung back.

"You sense my turmoil and you're here to offer wisdom, right?"

"Not really. The wisdom you need—"

"—is within me."

"No, it's within the dharma." He smiled. "The scent of all this pizza, it's beautiful, isn't it?"

We turned the corner and saw the Green up ahead, the dark illuminated by a circle of lanterns. Through the trees we could see the tents and the makeshift shelters, refrigerator boxes and tarps rigged up between the tents in a tight circle, a first-aid sign affixed to the largest structure. The Green was a public space; there were three port-o-johns along the perimeter and a bronze statue of George Washington by the entrance. It was past midnight and the camp was quiet, but as soon as we entered, someone pounded a drum, and a young guy in jeans and a hoodie emerged from the dark.

"Hey, the pizza monks are here," he shouted, and a few people came wandering out of their tents, blankets draped over their shoulders as they shuffled toward the food.

"I'm Clay. Thanks for the grub," the young guy said.

We shook hands as he led us to the dining hall—three picnic tables pushed together beneath an awning of clear plastic. The air held a crisp chill and Kasey huddled against me while the monks unloaded the pies.

The campers soon gathered, circling the tables as they grabbed slices and offered thanks.

Across the Green, I saw Phap Dong pacing alone in meditation, his head bowed, hands in a prayer position as he walked in a long, looping circle.

"Is he the one who gave you the poem?" Kasey asked. "That's why we're here, right? Go talk to him." She patted the car keys in her pants pocket. "If it gets too cold, I'll wait in the car."

"Come with me. Maybe it will help . . . "

"Go," she said, pecking my cheek, dismissing me.

Clay and some other dude lit up a joint after they scarfed down their slices, and I knew Kasey would join them once I stepped away, her old inclinations hard to shed.

Phap Dong looked up as I approached, slowing his pace until I joined him at the edge of the camp. The moonlight caught the sheen of his shaved head, a soft glow circling his crown. To his left, beside an old wooden bench, was a large red gas can, five gallons, enough to burn the whole encampment. Some of the gas must have spilled; the vapors cut through the night air.

"Flynn, I'm happy to see you," he said.

"Our menu promises free delivery."

"But not after ten," he smiled. "Others would have sent us to Pizza Hut. You have a beautiful heart."

"So they tell me. But it feels plug-ugly, most of the time."

"Walk with me," he said. "Sometimes the dharma finds us when we need it most."

I wasn't in the mood. "Are you really going to do this?"

"We'll know when it's done," he said. "My intention is good . . . but I'm scared shitless." He stopped pacing, reached into his robe and pulled out a cigarette, lighting up. "I quit four years ago. The cycles of samsara keep spinning."

"Don't do it," I said. "Walk away."

He took a long drag and exhaled through his nose.

"The monk Jinzang, many years ago, wrote that we offer our bodies to repay the Buddha's kindness, to pay homage to him, creating merit for all sentient beings. I was a prick before I found the dharma. I owe the Buddha everything. Perhaps, when people see what I've done, they'll be willing to take action. The Buddha teaches that the end of suffering is possible. People must know that."

"No one will learn a damn thing. They'll think you're crazy."

"Maybe I am. But if one person follows the path . . . maybe that one person is you, Flynn."

"Don't even go there. You ordered twenty pizzas and it's my job to make them. That's why I'm here."

"I'll be dead in a few hours. Don't lie to me, or yourself. Avoid that dishonor, please. That's not why you're here."

"Why did you give me that poem?" I asked.

"Because it's true. My body, this will be my offering. What will *you* offer, Flynn? You told me about your father once. In certain moments he's alive. In others he is dead. The same is true for all of us. Nothing is fixed. *Your vast shell reaches into endless space.*"

The moon threw shadows across the grass. Phap Dong flicked his cigarette toward the gas can, the ashes falling like dust. Across the Green, someone started playing guitar, the familiar chords of a song I knew but couldn't name. Phap Dong coughed twice and threw the cigarette to the ground.

"Now you feel how nothing clings to you," he said. "Find your pain and make an offering to it. *Your vast shell reaches into endless space.*"

"Where is this space you keep talking about? My whole life is a trap."

"You don't see it, but it is there. *I* didn't see it until I found the dharma. I'd still be banging teenagers in Thailand if I hadn't found it. Find your pain and make an offering."

He picked up the gas can and unscrewed the cap, inhaling the vapors, and for a moment I thought this was it, self-immolation, but after a few long, unsteady breaths he replaced the cap and sat down, crossing his legs and resting his hands on his knees, the gas can at his side. He closed his eyes and began to chant, a whisper as light as his breath.

I still had questions but he was done with me, his body stiff and corpse-like, his head facing the ground. I turned and headed back to the group.

As I reached the tents, the scent of marijuana grew strong, and, sure enough, Kasey was high. Years ago I'd smoked some, too, but quit after Dad shot himself. When I found his body there were three joints on the seat beside him. All those years together and I never suspected he smoked. The joints were spotted with blood and little specks of what I guessed were brain matter. Later, a friend offered to set the Honda on fire for the insurance money, but instead I washed the blood from the windshield and steam-cleaned the seats. Kasey and I still drove it. It was our only car.

In the days before Dad's suicide, it was just the two of us in a house in foreclosure, my father parked on the sofa staring at old sitcoms, a .38 and a box of bullets on the table next to his coffee mug, me half-baked, rushing off to Kasey's house to get stoned in the basement and screw to Arcade Fire. I never did a damn thing about the gun or those bullets; I just walked by day after day, as if they were a platter of saltines and Cheez Whiz. My father didn't leave a suicide note, but he did leave a single bullet in its regular place on the table, maybe hoping I would follow his lead. I still had it, tucked inside the toe of an old white sock in the back of a drawer. The police had kept the gun and those three bloody joints.

Back at the tables, I was greeted by two-thirds of Kasey's naked ass, her pants tugged down from her hips as she showed Clay and the monks her favorite tattoo, an elaborate garden of sunflowers and roses and long, flowing vines. Jersey Monk's stare made me want to slap him, but I knew Kasey enjoyed it, her exhibitionism stoked by a fresh joint and the attention of other men. Over the years, she'd cheated a few times and I wondered if the fetus—the baby: whatever you wanted to call it—was actually mine. It was an ugly thought, unfair; not that it mattered. We had an appointment at the clinic in less than eight hours.

Phap Dien approached and led me from the table. He touched my shoulder, and I waited for him to say something. But he remained silent, the steady pressure of his hand grounding me, and together we breathed. I heard Kasey giggling as she pulled up her pants and grabbed a final hit before coming over and leading me back to the pizza.

"Have a slice," she said. "I know the chef. He's cute."

At that moment I hated pizza. The night my father shot himself, I brought him two slices during my break—his last meal.

A serious-looking guy, clean-shaven in a baggy flannel shirt, walked over with a copy of Noam Chomsky's *On Anarchism*. He started talking about participatory democracy and alternate modes of production, the Mondragon co-op in Spain. He seemed worried we'd think the occupation wasn't serious, that it was all about hanging out and getting high.

"Read Sheldon Wolin and Rick Wolff," he said. "Read Antonio Gramsci. You can't understand the world until you understand Gramsci."

I asked Kasey if she was ready to leave. Jersey Monk hustled over and thanked me again for the pies.

"Tomorrow night, we'll be at the monastery, sitting in honor of Phap Dong. Please join us."

Across the Green, I saw Phap Dong seated beneath the oak tree, the gas can on his lap, his hands raised toward the sky.

Kasey and I said good-bye and started walking.

What will you offer, Flynn? Phap Dong had asked. I still had that Rilke poem folded in my pocket. *Nothing clings to you . . . your flesh, your fruit . . .* even my own child was a fleeting condition. Sometimes the only permanence I felt was that single leftover bullet in the back of my drawer.

We climbed into the Honda and I turned the key. Kasey reached over and stroked my hand.

"I'm sorry," she said. "I won't smoke anymore. That was the last time."

It was a lie; we both knew it, but I held on to her hand anyway, our warm breath forming vapor-ghosts across the windshield.

"You still want to do it, right?" I asked.

"Who knows . . . but I'm going to. Now is not the time. Maybe never, but certainly not now. We both know it."

On the dashboard, above the radio, was a divot where a bullet fragment had lodged into the dash. I'd pulled out the fragment but the hole had remained. When my father shot himself, the Honda, paid off the year before, was all he had left. Except me, who had done nothing to save him. With my free hand I touched the dashboard, pressed my thumb over the divot. At the time, one of the more tactless cops had suggested I junk the car, how with head wounds the shatter effect was too great: you could never find all the fragments.

Your flesh, your fruit . . . thick fluids rise and flow. Now you feel how nothing clings to you. Your vast shell reaches into endless space.

Find your pain and make an offering, Phap Dong had said.

I held on to the steering wheel but couldn't drive away, the windshield fog dissipating as the Honda grew warm. The divot on the dashboard—it was a vast, endless space.

"I'll be right back," I said.

Clay and the Chomsky-guy watched as I cut across the Green; the monks, pizza boxes in hand, heading after me as I hurried toward Phap

Dong. He was still seated with crossed legs, the gas can balanced on his lap, his right hand clutching the nozzle as he stared into the dark.

"I've been thinking about Medicine King," he said, his voice shaky and weak. "The Lotus Sutra explores his self-immolation, for the benefit of all sentient beings." He took a long, labored breath. "I wonder, before he lit the fire, if Medicine King wanted to throw up, too."

"Doesn't matter," I said, and reached for the gas can, grabbing the handle. "*This* is what I offer."

For a moment he resisted; then his grip released, his fingers falling from the nozzle as I pulled the can away from him. I waited for him to rise, to demand I give it back, but instead he unfolded his legs, stretched his arms, and burst out laughing.

"My intention remains," he said, breathing softly, "but thank you."

Jersey Monk handed him the last slice of pizza, and Phap Dong, smiling, wolfed it down.

"For the benefit of all sentient beings," I said, "or maybe just you and me."

Exhausted, I lugged the gas can back to my father's old Honda, emptied all five gallons into the tank, and hopped behind the wheel, Kasey snoring beside me as we drove into the night, into the vast, endless space.

Kate Fadick

after Maria Tsvetaeva

Tonight I want Hildegard's words

on the page
through my pen

lanterns left
in a hungry sky

a fearless river
with no grammar

song-filled hive
conjuring dark

honey for old wounds

an elegance
or blasphemy

it does not matter

Bad Apple

The red package is small and square but heavy, dense: when she presses it to her lips and breathes in slowly through her nose, she can smell rotting fruit.

Carefully, she sets it down on the countertop.

————

Bai Xue is having a dream that she lives in a fourth floor walk-up above an Indian restaurant.

In her dream, she bruises her knees and tortures her spine every day cleaning the homes of wealthy men who blame her for greasy fingerprints on their glass coffee tables. Then, every evening, when she arrives home after taking three different trains and walking for three blocks in her tennis shoes, the stairwell in her building is filled with the thick, boiling fog of spices that spills from the restaurant's loud kitchen. It makes her face run with sweat and tears and snot that she wipes away with the heels of her blistered hands as she unlocks her front door.

Three months ago, Bai Xue dreams, she was the most beautiful supermodel in the city. Now, exhausted, with blisters and stooped shoulders, she is the most beautiful cleaning lady in the world.

————

She can't pick off the packing tape with just her fingernails; she finds a knife in the silverware drawer and slices neatly through it. When she pulls back the box's flaps, she finds that the inside is stuffed with crimson and gold tissue paper.

————

In her dream, Bai Xue has roommates who always greet her warmly when she pushes open the heavy front door, wiping the mucus from her reddened upper lip. Amal is the son of the man who owns the building and the restaurant, and he is also the one who brought Bai Xue home in the first place. He has strong arms and a crooked face that twists up when he smiles; he is 4 feet 3 inches tall, coming up to Bai Xue's stomach. The other men who live in the apartment are

Amal's friends from the local dwarfism advocacy and support group. The tallest, Hassan, a saxophonist, is eye level with Bai Xue's breasts; Charlie, who paints, is smallest and comes up to her hip. Barry is a waiter; Karl and Paulo are unemployed; Henry is an actor who plays elves in Christmas specials; and Amal helps to run his parents' restaurant. Like all men Bai Xue has ever known, they are coarse and hungry, needy and easily wounded. Each night at dinner they sit in special high chairs around the big round wooden table in the kitchen and eat and drink beer and bellow, laughing over flipping-off some kid that stared at them funny on the A train that morning. At night, they sleep two-to-a-mattress to save space, curled up and facing away from each other.

———

Bai Xue dreams that these men allow her to stay on with them despite the fact that she has not been able to pay her full share of the rent once in the past three months. That they insist that she take one of the two bedrooms for herself, despite the fact that this means that every night one of them has to sleep on the living room floor. "The hardwood is good for our backs," Amal assures her. "You'll pay us back when you can," he reasons. His smile contorts his crooked face.

———

The tissue paper rustles as she lifts it out. It's perfectly round and heavy and smooth. A smooth surface cold enough to make the bones in her hands ache.

———

In Bai Xue's dream, it was Amal who had found her huddled on the frigid concrete sidewalk beside an ATM, her caked-on makeup smeared, wearing five-hundred-dollar jeans but no coat and no shoes in mid-November. Who had been close enough to the ground to look into her face and see that she wasn't a gaunt junkie with an endemic life story but something too perfect to allow to freeze to death on a dirty sidewalk. Who had taken her to his warm apartment and sat her on his couch and wrapped her in an afghan and brought her a soggy cardboard container of his mother's vindaloo pork, which was spicy enough to bring almost anyone back to life. Who had given her a place to live, helped her find steady work, coached her English from bad to okay. And who never asked, but let the unanswered questions hang like warm lanterns above their friendship, burning at them both, but only quietly.

Everything is very quiet as she looks down into her cupped hands.

———

Bai Xue dreams that it had been 2:00 a.m., long after the scalding white lights of the show, the razor-thin catwalk and the thudding electronic bassline out of time with her footsteps, and directly after the writhing coked out after party; her agent's friend, with rotting heavy breath, wouldn't unlock the car doors. Terror had made Bai Xue's entire body feel as weightless as Styrofoam; trembling, she had licked her lips and looked into his eyes, slid to the floor of the car on her knees between his legs and told him that she wanted just what he wanted. And then, as he leaned back and she leaned forward, she had very suddenly turned her head and like a vicious desperate animal bit down on his inner thigh hard enough to make him double over with a shriek as she got the door unlocked and scrambled outside and ran.

Even with all their paternal kindness, Bai Xue thinks maybe her roommates would be just the same, if they possibly could. At night she can hear them moaning for her, but she does not lock her door while she sleeps because she knows that they know that she knows that not one of them has a body capable of hurting her in the way that strong, big men sometimes hurt beautiful young girls. Daily, at breakfast and just before bed, she can see the primal humiliation of it in their eyes.

———

She lifts it to her lips and rests them on its surface, like a distracted kiss. Again, the smell of fermentation. Her mouth fills with saliva.

———

There is one night when Amal smells like cigarette smoke and curry and liquor as he clambers into her bed like a child coming to sleep with his parents after a bad nightmare. He whimpers as he presses his hips up against her, a pathetic plea, and Bai Xue gives him the flat of her hand, not squeezing or stroking but a simple steadiness, for him to rub himself against. It takes around seven minutes and in the end he clings and weeps an apology into her breast and she studies the dark ceiling and breathes the smell of curry on his skin and thinks that the good men are the ones who only want to fuck their mothers.

———

It tastes like candy but it turns into glass in her throat.

Karen Hopper
CONTRIBUTING EDITOR

LOCAL PROFILE: LANSING, MI

Capital City Writers Association

CAPITAL CITY WRITERS ASSOCIATION

There probably aren't a lot of professions in the world where you don't have colleagues. For writers and other creative types, however, the early years spent working on your craft can be lonely. In the popular imagination, "introvert" and "writer" go hand-in-hand, but despite what internet memes will tell you, even the most introverted of writers will have moments where face-to-face human interaction helps them move forward creatively.

For writers in mid-Michigan, that's where the Lansing-based Capital City Writers Association comes in handy. The nearly three-year-old organization now has over ninety dues-paying members and a robust board of directors (I am one).

Advice for career-changers almost always includes "join a professional organization," and it is advice many people take. National organization Romance Writers of America has more than 10,000 members and dozens of local chapters. CCWA president and founder Louise Knott Ahern is an RWA member, but wanted to form a local, genre-agnostic writer's organization to bust the echo-chamber.

"If we're just starting out as writers, sometimes we don't really know where we're going. We just know we have stories we want to tell . . . " says Ahern. Putting writers from diverse genres together helps keep everybody's horizons broad and their perspectives in check. CCWA gives its members an opportunity to commiserate, to share their dreams, and to hold each other, if not exactly accountable, then at least goal-oriented.

One of the most important ways CCWA helps keep writers focused on their objectives is through their flagship Finish the Damn Book program. FTDB is both in-person and online. Monthly workshops are dedicated to specific craft and publishing questions, while informal write-ins give people the chance to practice their craft elbow-to-elbow with other people who don't mind if you look up all of a sudden and ask how to spell "cunnilingus." Wednesday night virtual write-ins are mostly through Facebook, with FTDB leaders issuing word-count goals and words of encouragement. Members of the Facebook group share links about writing and ask for advice on plotting, character development, and diabolical ways to kill people off.

CCWA leaders dream of taking FTDB national in the coming years and see the program as a complement, not a competitor to National Novel Writing Month. Ahern says for many members, NaNoWriMo is the last push they need to finish the damn book.

Once that book is finished (and even if it's not), CCWA members have the option of getting discounted admission to the organization's yearly conference, Write on the Red Cedar (named for the river flowing through Michigan State University's campus). The 2016 conference returns to the Kellogg Center on MSU's campus in East Lansing January 22nd and 23rd. This year's headliner was literary agent Donald Maass; in 2016 it will be *New York Times* bestseller Bob Mayer.

If "*New York Times* bestseller" seems like a distinctly commercial sentiment for a writer's conference, that's deliberate. Ahern is a journalist with twenty years of experience, and her conviction infuses the organization with this belief: writers deserve to get paid.

"The creative product is every bit as valuable as any other product that somebody with skills and expertise produces," says Ahern. "That's why, for CCWA, an underlying theme and mission of ours is for people to become professional writers—and part of that is making people realize: what you do, you deserve to be paid for."

Catherine Moore

Road to Nowhere

"OK girls, hang a right at the end of the drive. It's 'bout three minutes up on the left-hand side."

With an OHV engine jolt they twist tires in the mud and career away from the fish camp, this Thelma and gal pal waving gleefully from inside a convertible tank of a Cadillac.

"Take care of my baby," his shouted afterthought.

Out on Highway 90, the stick of a girl, swallowed by a baggy purple sweater, searches her purse and pulls out a roll as reedy thin as the swamp grass flying by, lights, and drags. She tips back her head in the passenger seat to watch clouds flicker as she waits for the exhale.

Three tokes, then she slides herself across the bench seat, next to her auburn-haired friend.

"Can't..."

"Can!" She holds the hand-rolled butt up to the driver's mouth for her to inhale, as the car churns down the empty center line of the road.

"Oooow!" Her dark purple arm reaches around the redhead to hold her in a hug. Together they scream and sing along to The Cure's "Mint Car." Not a note of concern passing the mile marker attached with *Leaving St. Tammany Parish,* because the perfect sun is still up, and there is nowhere they'd rather be than watching the vanilla bayou, lit all bounce and kiss on the passing wetlands.

Welcome to Mississippi is the sign that finally slows the V8 engine: "Damn, girl, I think we are going the wrong way."

"*Merde,*" a moment of serious reflection before hysterical bursts into the silent swamp. The Caddie fishtails in rhythm with their waves of laughter. *Chuggle, chuggle, chuggle,* the 1957 convertible wavers, lurches, chokes, and slowly glides off on the soft shoulder amid reeds and more pinches of laughter.

The Dixie beer run forgotten, the evening suddenly becomes about setting strawberry-colors over bayou waters, the space of a warm hood on a big Cadillac, and friends wrapped in each other's embrace.

Marwyck

I wear myself out keeping myself calm
—Barbara Stanwyck

I can love them all, now,
because what does it matter?
A chemical in the brain
makes time spin faster.
The rolling wheel of aftermath
loses heat as it tumbles
down the dell.

A Christmas card
my mother bought
is my memory palace,
all the elves asleep
in a row of beds
on a travertine balcony
above the hearth.

Let's pin it down
to blueprints. How much
closer can we get to living?
Stanwyck built a castle
in the Southern California desert
and made it look like
Camelot.

She rode the train
from Hollywood
to seventy years ago.
When FDR pressed a button
in the White House,
confetti rained down
on Omaha.

I bet God will understand
the smallness of my wants.
In the middle of summer
I miss summer.
Marwyck will be my heaven.
I've peopled it already
with ghosts of the living.

Cut and Run

It can be deceitful, deceptive
when a colony of bees
completely abandons its hive
doesn't tell anyone, just goes
has committed what appears
to be an unlawful theft
skirted the joint
and gone
left the honey still dripping
from the comb
mid-moment
and gone
hive still hanging
now like a thrown hat
caught close to the sky.
What now.
Now the bees are gone
absconded bees
paraphrasing a murder
mystery, the crows are
watching, eyes popping
like music, cawing, this
fat winter kill has us all
but the bees
who have gone
sold like a ring on an outbound
train; cut and run.
The hat is shivering lightly
or there is a wind
or a car has passed and made
some but not all of the world
move in its wake.

Dustin Keate

Camaraderie of Proximity

The family of strangers I grew up with, went to church with, went to grade school, senior high, and college with, are a dimming part of me. I enlisted in the Army and disappeared. Sometimes an old friend will reach me with an impersonal and flat "Happy Birthday" on social media, but I don't respond. As the years go by, my old families contact me less as I fade into sand and join a new family, one born of necessity.

My new family is a foster home. New brothers walk through it and I connect with some. We share war stories, we share drinks, and we share proximity. With those I feel most comfortable with, I share my story. But eventually all of them leave my home and move to another. Wards of the state, we do not move ourselves—we are moved.

My present foster home is a tent in Iraq. Proximity in a tent is inexorable and solitude only exists when sitting in a portable toilet. I'm here with some of the best men I've ever known. They are rugged, effective, and determined. I've shared everything with them. Twice probably. We are family. However, even this family will fade. I'll become "a guy they knew," they'll become "my team in Iraq."

We drink together, sitting in our tent, speaking vulgarities. We talk about our unenviable lives. We lust for a cure and find it in talk about women and wild nights. We pass around a Listerine bottle with illicit whiskey inside, smuggled into the country in a care package labeled toiletries. The rim is gritty from the dry, fissured lips before mine. The liquid inside is bottom shelf—special reserve is too remarkable for our weathered tent.

One of us pulls out a tablet and finds pictures of an ex-girlfriend. "She was batshit crazy, but awesome in bed," he brags. He shows us a photo of her, from back when they were together, and a photo of her now. The pictures are seven years apart, but the difference is about twenty years and thirty pounds. He pulls up another set of pictures. "This guy was the badass in high school," he tells us. On the screen is an obese, unemployed burnout that lives in an unkempt room at his mom's house. A few more of us indulge in the voyeuristic schadenfreude. A drug-addicted cousin's selfie, taken in the mirror he cuts lines on, an ex-girlfriend-turned-stripper's escort profile, a recent DUI mug shot of a deadbeat dad. We try to find the best worst humans we know.

I decide to try finding my own antidote to my drunken deployment depression by looking at the dour lives of people from my past. I went to a small private school in West Texas. I start with my graduating class. The men I'm with know my story and where I came from. People said I had natural talent for the sciences. I was destined for greatness. Instead, I dropped out of university, then a community college, until eventually, stuck in a sinking roundabout of terminal jobs, I decided to find experience and maybe a modicum of discipline in the Army. I stumbled, but I am better; I will certainly find a wealth of fodder for the evening's entertainment.

I start with my high school's quarterback. He looks fit, works in the oil business, has a beautiful home and a beautiful wife. I try again. I find a world traveler with a graduate degree in photography and a job with National Geographic. Again. A university professor. I find a doctor in the bunch. A writer, a successful actor, a few more oil businessmen and doctors, an Air Force pilot, a politician, and a business owner. And every single one shares pictures of opulent weddings, expensive European adventures, and all the model markers of success in modern life.

"Dude, you're the loser! You're the fuckup!" My temporary family laughs. I laugh, too, but it stings to realize that I am another person's antidote to a missed promotion. If an ex-girlfriend feels like her life is a stagnant puddle, she just looks at what she got away from, and just in time, too. I hand off the tablet and retreat to the only place I can be alone, the steamy portable toilet. Seated over a mound of shit, I hold my head in my hands and shed a few tears alongside my laughter. I am weight gain underneath a repugnant tattoo. I am a bloody-nosed mug shot, a vomit-covered pair of skinny jeans.

I dab my eyes with my sleeve, take a deep breath through my nose, leave my fetid fortress, and shout out, "Specialist Perkins, I bet you stuck your dick in Crazy, let's see her now!" I take another drink from the shared bottle and laugh with my team in Ramadi.

David James Poissant

David James Poissant is an award-winning writer whose stories and essays have appeared in *The Atlantic, The Chicago Tribune, Ploughshares, The Southern Review, One Story, Playboy, The New York Times,* and the *New Stories from the South* and *Best New American Voices* anthologies. Recently, David graciously agreed to serve as Guest Judge of *The Indianola Review*'s $1,000 Leap Day Flash Fiction Contest. *Indianola Review* staffer Geosi Gyasi picks David's brain on the craft, the industry, his personal literary ambitions, and, of course, what David will be looking out for when selecting our grand prize winner.

GEOSI GYASI

Lauren Groff, author of *Arcadia* and National Book Award Finalist for her novel *Fates and Furies,* has said you're "one of our finest young writers, with a taut and subtle prose style, a deep knowledge of craft, and a heart so vast it encompasses whole worlds." Do you think you deserve all this praise from the literary community? Has it altered your approach?

DAVID JAMES POISSANT

I suppose there's no good way to answer that question. If I say that I believe I deserve the praise, I sound vain. If I say that I don't deserve it, I risk sounding falsely modest. I suppose that I can only answer honestly and admit that I have no idea. It's all happened so fast, it feels a little bewildering. Though it's taken me ten years to get here, it still feels like it's happened rather quickly. Plus, I don't think that any artist has a firm understanding of his or her own place in the grand scheme of things. I'm just happy to be here. I'm happy that my work speaks to readers. If some of those readers happen to be other writers, I'm happy about that too.

GEOSI

What sparked your journey to becoming a writer?

DAVID

Becoming a writer, for many, means leaving behind this very American sense of security and financial well-being. I was twenty-six years old when I really committed to being a writer. My wife and I were stable. We owned a home with only twenty-seven years left on the mortgage. We had good jobs with good pensions. We had our whole lives planned. Indeed, had we stuck with it, we could have retired in our fifties. Then, I had to go and mess it all up by wanting to become a writer, which meant quitting our jobs, selling our house, and moving across the country for grad school, then across the country again for more grad school, then navigating a ruthless academic job market and a publishing industry that seldom favors literary fiction. I've been very fortunate, but it definitely could have gone all wrong.

GEOSI

Is there anything you wanted to do besides write?

DAVID

Yes, I grew up on comic books, and I always thought I'd be a comic illustrator. Short of that, I was sure I'd do something in the visual arts or something with graphic design. I still love to draw and sketch, and book design is very important to me.

GEOSI

Did you have a hand in the cover design of your book *The Heaven of Animals?*

DAVID

I didn't have a hand in the design itself, but my editor gave me more leeway than most authors get in rejecting a number of potential designs that I didn't care for. The one we landed on was the one that we both agreed was best for the book.

GEOSI

How about a technical question for our readers, many of whom are writers themselves.

What are the main technical or stylistic tools you consider vital to your work?

DAVID

Great question! If by technical, you mean what makes it tick, I believe that most good stories benefit from a beginning, middle, and end. I like stories that don't resolve too neatly with a cherry on top but which, nevertheless, answer the question or questions the reader's been reading for. I believe that a story teaches the reader how to read it. If a story announces itself as realism, it's a rare story that can shift to magic realism successfully on the last page. Finally, I try to make the act of reading easy on my readers. While the narratives may challenge, and while I may experiment with point of view shifts, etc., I try to obey most conventional rules of grammar and punctuation. There are some writers I love, Cormac McCarthy among them, who write dialogue minus quotation marks, but I've never found a way to do that half as well as he does. I worry about losing a reader along the way. So, I try to stick to the basics of punctuation. Maybe, as I get older and wiser, I'll take more risks in that department.

GEOSI

I'm intrigued that you mentioned Cormac McCarthy, who of course has a unique style of writing. In an interview with Oprah Winfrey, he once said he prefers "simple declarative sentences." Would you consider your own sentences style simplistic, or more complex? In other words, how would you typically describe the mechanics of your sentences?

DAVID

That's interesting. I can't speak for McCarthy, but when I read a book like *Blood Meridian* or *Suttree*, "simple and declarative" are not the adjectives that come to mind. Some of his sentences are simple, sure, but most are lush and lyrical and meandering in the best kind of way. As for my own sentence structure, I like variety. Generally, the greater the number of independent clauses and prepositional phrases and appositives, the more complex the sentence becomes.

GEOSI

Who are your literary precursors? Which writers or teachers have had the greatest impact on your work as a writer?

DAVID

In terms of teachers, I owe a lot to Bret Anthony Johnston, who has been a mentor and cheerleader from early on. Jack Riggs taught me a great deal about close reading. Sandra Meek, a poet, encouraged me long before I knew any fiction writers. Then, at the University of Arizona, I learned a great deal from Aurelie Sheehan and Jason Brown. Later, at the University of Cincinnati, I had the pleasure of working with Leah Stewart, Michael Griffith, and Brock Clarke, from whom I also learned much. You can't repay your teachers. You just can't. So, I teach students of my own as a way of repayment. I hope those students will go on to help the next generation of writers, and so on.

GEOSI

Let's dive into your process a bit. Would you agree that short stories are easier to write, generally, than novels?

DAVID

I don't know that that's true. Some beginning writers may think that stories are easier to write, but both forms have their own unique challenges. In my experience, the differences between a story and a novel are as significant as the differences between a sonnet and an epic poem. The differences transcend length. Novels take much longer to write than a story, but many novels are written more quickly than story collections, if that makes sense. It took me eight years to write enough good stories to fill a book of stories. I finished the first draft of my novel in three years. While the novel is just a lot of book to write, you have the advantage of a single narrative arc and the pleasure of working with the same characters for years at a time.

GEOSI

How do you discover your characters as you write? Before you begin or as the story unfolds?

DAVID

I don't discover a character until I'm deep into the middle of his or her story. Sometimes I reach the end of a story never quite having discovered a character. Often, characters—their motivations, their fears, their hopes, their dreams—don't shine through until revision.

GEOSI

Interesting. Speaking of revision, how many times do you revise your drafts? At what point do you consider a story ready for outside eyes?

DAVID

Every story calls for something different. Occasionally, I write a story in a day or two, and, when I'm done, the story's nearly done. I put it in a drawer for a month, I pull it out, I put a coat of polish on it, and I send the story out. Often, though, a story takes weeks to write and years to get right.

GEOSI

What do you do when you hit a wall in a story?

DAVID

Sometimes I'll plow through and force an ending. Sometimes this works, and sometimes it ruins the story. Other times, I'll put the story away for a few months and work on something else until I think up an ending. Sometimes this works, and sometimes I lose track of the voice that drew me into the story altogether. For every story I've finished and published, there are several companion pieces that have yet to find their middles and/or their ends.

GEOSI

"The Disappearing Boy," published in The Good Men Project and later in *The Heaven of Animals*, features an ending I find quite intriguing: "I never saw Chris again. After that day, he disappeared. In this way, we both lived up to our namesakes." Did you see Chris disappearing even as you began the story?

DAVID

Definitely not. That ending surprised me as well.

GEOSI

Is it always your aim to surprise readers with the way you end your stories?

DAVID

I like endings that, as Flannery O'Connor put it, feel somehow both surprising *and* inevitable.

GEOSI

How important is the relationship between reading and writing? Do you regard yourself as a voracious reader?

DAVID

I guess by most standards, I'm a pretty voracious reader. I read about a book a week. I used to read almost a book a day. But, I had kids, and, now, I also have a full-time teaching job, and I write a lot. So, I don't get to read as much as I used to. It's funny, a year ago, I met a Pulitzer Prize winner. I was nervous meeting him. He asked me the same question, and, when I told him I read a book a week, he said that was too fast, that I should slow down and savor every page. This year, I had the good fortune of meeting another Pulitzer Prize winner, and, when he asked me your question, and I said "a book a week," he shook his head and said, "Come on, now, you can do better than that." I hold both these men, and their fiction, in high esteem. But, it just goes to show you, there's no one right way to be a good reader or a good writer.

GEOSI

I know oftentimes that a story begins with an idea, unless perhaps, you disagree with me. Where did the titular story of your collection, *The Heaven of Animals*, come from?

DAVID

The title story is a sequel, of sorts, to the first story in the collection, "Lizard Man." Those are the only stories that are explicitly linked. I returned to the character Dan Lawson only because, a few years after

"Lizard Man" was published, I felt that Dan and I had unfinished business. The end of any story is never really the end of the story. Well, *Hamlet* may be an exception. Once all of the characters are dead, I guess that's the end of the story. But, in Dan's case, I wondered what happened to the father and son years later. From there, it was a matter of getting Dan across the country and, scene by scene, deciding what he'd find along the way. The challenge of that story was in writing an episodic almost-novella-length piece that still felt as though it had a unifying narrative thread. Never losing track of that thread was important to me. Despite all of the adventures along the way, I wanted the story to always be about Dan getting to his son. David Lynch's film *The Straight Story* was a helpful model for me in writing the piece.

GEOSI

What are your literary ambitions? What does the future hold?

DAVID

I'm finishing a novel right now for Simon & Schuster. I have ideas aplenty for several novels after this, and I probably have enough stories for a second collection. I also hope to put together a collection of essays, one of these days. I've been writing a number of pieces about faith and about my sad, weird Southern Baptist upbringing. I'd need to give that project more focus, but I can foresee a time when I might have a memoir or collection about growing up in the church and my subsequent explorations of faith.

GEOSI

I nearly forgot: Do you mind giving me a brief insight into your forthcoming novel from Simon & Schuster?

DAVID

Absolutely. There are two stories in the collection, "Venn Diagram" and "Wake the Baby," that concern the characters Lisa and Richard Starling. I wrote the first story not thinking there would be a second, and I wrote the second not thinking there would be a third. In time, the third became the novel I'm finishing now. I could not let go of those characters. I wondered where they wound up thirty years after the events of "Wake the Baby." The novel concerns three days in the lives of Lisa, Richard, and their grown sons, Michael and Thad, as well as Michael's wife, Diane, and Thad's boyfriend, Jake. The six have come together for a last week at the family lake house before the house is sold and Richard and Lisa retire to Florida. As you may know, whenever family gets together for more than three days, things have a tendency to get ugly, and the world of this novel is no exception.

GEOSI

You're the guest judge for the inaugural flash fiction contest organized by *The Indianola Review*. My question is, what will you be looking for in our finalists' work? What will help you choose your winner?

DAVID

A good short-short story is not a scene from a longer work or an unfinished story. Flash fiction is no more a failed form of the short story than a story is a failed novel. This is to say that a good short-short should have a beginning, a middle, and an end. The best pack all of the emotional wallop of a novel into two or three pages!

GEOSI

Let's close with a tangent in honor of *The Heaven of Animals*. Do you have any pets? Any fond memories of childhood pets?

DAVID

I have a beloved fourteen-year-old Chihuahua, Scooter. We also have a fish tank in the house. I love to keep angelfish. My daughters each have a goldfish. And, growing up, I had just about every pet a boy could have. This includes, but is not limited to, mice, hamsters, gerbils, a guinea pig, parakeets, a snake, frogs, fish, turtles, hermit crabs, a dog, a cat, and a rabbit. (Not all at once.)

GEOSI

Animals play major thematic roles in your debut collection of short stories. I have to ask: Why animals?

DAVID

I fell in love with animals long before I found them to be promising subjects for my fiction. I don't quite know how it happens. Often, I joke that when I don't know where to take a story next, I either make two characters have sex or I have an animal enter the scene. I have yet to combine those strategies.

———

DAVID JAMES POISSANT's writing has been awarded the Matt Clark Prize, the George Garrett Fiction Award, the RopeWalk Fiction Chapbook Prize, the GLCA New Writers Award, and the Alice White Reeves Memorial Award from the National Society of Arts & Letters. He's the author of a short story collection, *The Heaven of Animals*, published by Simon & Schuster in 2014, and is currently at work on a novel. For more, visit davidjamespoissant.com.

GEOSI GYASI is a librarian, book blogger, reader, writer, and interviewer. He has interviewed over 300 writers and poets across the world, including Nobel Prize recipient Roald Hoffmann, Commonwealth Prize winner Benjamin Kwakye, Orange Prize winner Irene Sabatini, Caine Prize winner Henrietta Rose-Innes, Penguin Prize for African Writing winner Ellen Banda-Aaku, and Poet Laureate of Rhode Island Emeritus Tom Chandler. His work has appeared in *Visual Verse, Verse-Virtual, The New Black Magazine, Misty Review, Nigerians Talk, African Writer,* and others. He blogs at www.geosireads.wordpress.com.

Keith Lesmeister

The Birds Will Tell You What Happens Next
or
Stray Goats

Near the fifth anniversary of his parents' passing, Vincent's grandfather showed him an article in the *Iowa Today*—a section of newspaper dedicated to the comings and goings of Eastern Iowa. Stray goats had been spotted by hikers in a large swath of timber that butted-up against the Cedar River, not far from where they lived. The article alleged that one or more of the goats had showed signs of aggression. Vincent's grandfather laughed at the news, said there was no such thing as violent goats. Only gawkers and journalists who wanted a story.

The southwest edge of Cedar Rapids had yet to be fully developed, though contractors were starting to purchase acres of land, clear cutting trees. Still, it had a remote feel—just a couple clusters of trailer homes and small houses grouped together to make up a few shabby neighborhoods. There were newer housing options, but those were closer to the shopping malls and gas stations.

Word at the bait shop was the goats had been wandering through yards near the river, foraging for food, uprooting gardens: potatoes, kale, carrots, beets—cool-weather crops. His grandfather wanted to track them. Hunt them down. Vincent was fourteen.

"Get the .22 and .410 ready," his grandfather said, biting into a piece of peanut butter toast.

"We're gonna shoot them?" Vincent said.

"Shoot and eat," his grandfather said. "Thanksgiving feast."

Vincent looked at his paper plate; it was dirty enough to throw away. He crumpled it, tossed it in the garbage, and set his coffee mug in the sink. The idea of tracking stray goats didn't sit well with him. The idea of tracking something domestic-turned-wild sent nervous tremors through his stomach and legs.

This was early November, and the wind had already shifted from the northwest, bringing with it a seasonal chill, a sign of winter. Tree limbs were bare, the land a dull brown. Vincent loved this time of year: the cool, crisp air, the football games, the pumpkin pies—the entirety of which he and his grandfather could eat in one sitting.

"That paper plate," his grandfather said, pointing in the trash, "was clean enough to use again. Pay attention, will you? You're not the one shelling out dough for groceries and plates." He took his last bite of toast.

Vincent nodded.

When he was younger, his grandfather used to beat him with a rubber hose if he wasted too much food or kept the fridge door open too long. Now that he was older, he was beaten rarely, if ever, but the tone of his grandfather's voice was sharp, demeaning. It seemed his grandfather was always finding ways to harp on him.

"I'll get the rifle and shotgun and meet you in the garage," Vincent said.

His grandfather traversed these wooded hills as a younger man, back when it was still out of the city limits. The city had since rezoned to include tracts of this land, but that wouldn't stop his grandfather from using a gun in city limits.

The forest came right up to the road, giving it a cave-like feel. The gray sky hung low. Vincent cracked his window for fresh air. It smelled of burning leaves. They pulled into a dirt parking lot just off the gravel road, usually reserved for hikers and fishermen.

"I'm gonna drop you off at one end of the abandoned orchard," his grandfather said.

"Orchard?" Vincent said.

His grandfather gripped the steering wheel with both hands. "Hardly anyone knows about it, or even who planted it," his grandfather said. "It's rumored some river rat who lived in a shanty not far from here put in all these apple and pear trees since he didn't have land of his own. Probably dead now. No one tends to it. It's basically just a feeding ground for deer. The orchard's up there—you can't see it from here." His grandfather pointed up the steep embankment. A bed of leaves coated most of the hill. Only the oak trees still held a few rust-colored leaves.

"Do you think we could stick together?" Vincent said. "I don't know my way around here."

"You'll be fine," his grandfather said. "Just do as I say. I'll come through the woods and find you."

Goats roaming through the countryside weren't an uncommon occurrence. They got loose all the time, but it was rarely reported. The farmers would usually just rally up the strays and no harm would be done. What wasn't common, now, as the paper reported, was that some of the goats were rumored to be mean and aggressive, charging at hikers and dogs. This was more than likely the lone, feral goat—a wily male who'd escaped years ago and had somehow survived. Hardly anyone saw him, but stories were crafted every year that added to his mystique: that he'd killed small dogs, chased kids, knocked over garbage cans, and was once reported attacking hikers. Vincent was thinking of this as he and his grandfather hopped out of the van.

"I used to take your dad out here," his grandfather said. It surprised Vincent to hear this. They rarely—if ever—talked about his dad, his grandparents' only son. "We used to hike in the hills, or sometimes we'd snag carp in the river." Vincent's parents had died in a car collision in Iowa City, twenty miles south. That year they'd gotten an early snowfall, a heavy wet snow that brought out the plows. Vincent knew, from hearing his father talk, that it's always tricky navigating the early storms, like trying to relearn roller-skating as an adult. The plow had broadsided them. They were reported dead upon impact. After the funeral, his grandfather didn't speak to anyone for days, weeks. And his grandmother, now deceased, sobbed continuously.

"Take this logging road," his grandfather said. It was indeed a logging trail, but it was overgrown with tawny grasses and knee-high shrubs. "It'll lead you to a clearing. Position yourself on the south end—"

"I don't know which way—"

"Figure it out for chrissake," his grandfather said. "Use some common sense." He handed Vincent the .22. Vincent checked the safety, as he'd been taught to do upon accepting a weapon. "Load it." His grandfather handed him a box of shells.

"We're in city limits," Vincent said. He looked around. He thought he heard a vehicle coming up on them. He looked back.

Nothing.

"You don't know which way is south, but you know where the city's drawn its lines?" His grandfather laughed, but not in a friendly way. "Don't be a smartass. Load the rifle and start walking." He pointed into the woods. "Position yourself against a tree. Wear this." He handed him a blaze orange stocking cap. "I'll be wearing one, too. Don't shoot at anything unless you know what it is. Don't shoot a deer, a squirrel; don't shoot anything unless it's a goat."

"I've never really shot one of these," Vincent said, fumbling with the shells, trying to pry them into the magazine. He'd cut his thumb and was bleeding a little, but he didn't say anything. He was mostly used to small-gauge shotguns.

"Just like your pellet gun," his grandfather said. "No kick. A little louder, but no kick. Lean into your shot. Steady your breath, and squeeze the trigger." Vincent continued loading shells into the magazine. "Hurry up," his grandfather said, looking down the sights of the .410 shotgun, eyeing the bare branches of oaks and maples and ash trees. Vincent felt an insecure power while holding the small-caliber rifle. Like his entire life could be changed with one shot.

"How long?" Vincent said. "How long until I see you?" It wasn't cold, but he felt himself shivering. He needed to use a bathroom.

"Just position yourself on the south end, against a tree, and face north. I'll be walking up from the river through the woods and into the field. I'll be working slow, because I don't want to spook those goats if they're up there. I imagine they're either bedded down, grazing, or gnawing on those apples that've already dropped. They could be feasting under those trees."

"What if one comes after me?"

"They won't," he said.

"That lone stray—"

"Shoot the damn thing and you won't have to worry about it."

"What are we going to do with it?"

"Is this twenty questions, for chrissake?" His grandfather turned and started toward his side of the van. "Thanksgiving dinner," he said. "That's what we're going to do with it."

Vincent paced up the hill, finding a game trail to follow. It was hard dirt, narrow, clear of any leaves or brush. The hill was steep, and he found himself sweating under his quilted flannel, breathing hard.

He wondered how his grandfather would traverse this slope. He wasn't overweight, but he didn't move well—arthritic knees and feet. And trouble breathing.

Vincent kept his head up, aware of every noise and leaf and twig and acorn that rustled the forest floor. As he climbed higher onto the ridge, the clouds parted, showing a pale sky. When he reached the top of the trail he took off his heavy flannel, flung it over his shoulder. Just as his grandfather had said, there was an old, scraggily orchard with red fruit piled underneath the trees. Some apples still clung to the branches. Blue jays screeched. The sky continued to open and Vincent felt the sun's warmth on his face. He swatted at box-elder bugs landing on his arms. The air smelled of fermented apples. He scanned the area, wondered for a moment which direction was north, south. His grandfather's notion of "common sense" was never what Vincent had in mind. He looked up, trying to predict the trajectory of the sun. He located a sugar maple at the edge of the field. He imagined it was the south end. As his grandfather instructed, he shuffled over to the tree, leaned against it—big and towering, it stood higher than the rest. He found comfort against the maple, waiting, eyeing the field, the orchard, for movement. But for a long time there was nothing.

After a while he knelt on the ground, then sat. His nervous edge wore off, and he found himself exhausted. He dozed in and out of sleep. The slightest rustle or birdsong startled him conscious. Then he'd again scan the field, the apple trees. Birds sang from their camouflage branches, squirrels hauled away whole apples.

It occurred to him as he rested against the maple, the forest at his back, orchard and field out in front, that his father would've loved this adventure. Sure, it was technically illegal, and sure, they might be shooting at some farmer's goats, but his father loved an adventure and the kind of reckless fun that would, if anything, bring harm only to the adventurer, no one else. In other words, he would've loved to have hunted stray goats. Thinking about that offered Vincent no sense of contentment, waves of nervousness spread through his stomach and legs as he spotted movement on the north side. An animal working its way around the edge of the field.

When Vincent was eight, on a summer night just over a year before his parents' accident, he and his father, with some of the boys from the neighborhood, streaked through the alley, diving behind cars and trees, pulling metal lids off trash cans, using them as shields. Everyone carried two squirt guns and used random outdoor faucets to refill their weapons.

Once, he and his father ducked behind a garage, hiding from the teenage boys who were stalking each other, tiptoeing around vehicles and side yards. "Watch those bushes, Vinnie," his dad had told him. "Watch for the birds. They're our warning. You'll see them fly out before a person passes." His dad squatted next to him holding one red and one blue squirt gun. He winked at him, smiled. He sprayed Vincent's arm with a friendly shot of water, and said, "The birds will tell you what happens next."

Now, up against the maple, he focused on the animal, eyes wide and watery. He blinked and momentarily lost the image. He adjusted his back against the tree. He scanned the area across the orchard, searching for a color or slight movement to help him re-engage. Asian beetles landed on his neck, startling him. He barely noticed the wave of birds fluttering past him, hovering, dipping, sputtering around bushes, stopping to perch and glance and then fly again. This meant his grandfather was pushing up the far hillside. But he couldn't see him or, at this point, the animal, which had to be a goat. He brought the gun out in front of him, rested it on his knee.

He waited. More birds. Spooked flocks of blue jays, grackles, and redwing blackbirds that were out pecking at seeds and bugs. Next came a deer, a buck whose coat had lost that summer shine. It was now a dull, grayish brown. A small, six-point rack. It trotted from one side of the field to the other, tail up, toward the woods. He brought the .22 to his shoulder and looked down the barrel, taking aim at the vital area of the deer, a place that both his father and grandfather taught him to aim for. "A deer won't survive a shot in the vitals," his dad had said, circling the area on the life-size target. "You don't have to hit the heart," he said. "Lungs are fine, too." A deer wouldn't survive a lung-shot, which made the critical circle around the vitals much larger. While Vincent possessed this information, he'd never had a chance to use it. Never took aim, never pulled the trigger on an animal so big. His heart hammered inside his chest. His breathing was erratic. He stood up and right away cursed himself because the goat—yes, it was a goat—skipped right for him. But it wasn't in any hurry. It hadn't seen him. And because of this—because he had time to watch and think about his shot, because he thought this might be the wily male that had been allegedly charging people, and because he was now standing and wouldn't have a steady shot—Vincent grew anxious. His heartbeat continued pounding. Something rushed into his throat. He could barely breathe.

The goat stopped under a single oak tree about thirty yards away—the tree's crooked, scraggily branches twisting in all directions. Vincent calmed and tried to think clearly. Where was his grandfather? Where was his blaze orange hunting cap? He should be walking out of the woods at any second, which meant he couldn't take aim and shoot in that direction. He'd have to wait for the goat to run to the side, around him.

The goat began hop-running toward him. Tall and confident, almost regal. He brought the gun to his shoulder. The goat wasn't big, but it was smart, wary, and its demeanor made it seem larger than it was. He observed that its white fur looked dulled, probably from the elements, and its horns grew up and straight back. Vincent found himself in awe of the beast. He felt sure that this was the one.

Pretty soon, behind the single goat, came the rest of the trip. Maybe six, seven. They hurried directly at him. The leader, the lone goat, came to within twenty yards, but still no sign of his grandfather.

The shot was within range, but he didn't feel comfortable taking it. The butt of the gun was still against his shoulder, and his arms were getting tired. He brought the rifle down to his side; the goat must've noticed the movement, because it snapped its head in his direction and took two hard leaps toward him. Vincent's heart thumped. The goat brought one of its front legs up, then stomped the ground. A violent thud, a territorial warning. It snorted, lowered and raised its head. They locked eyes, and it stomped again. Vincent's arms were numb, paralyzed. The goat took two more assertive lunges toward him, and Vincent lost his cool, brought the gun up to his shoulder. The movement sent the goat cantering to the edge of the field. Vincent didn't have time to think. The .22 cracked the air, causing his right ear to ring. The goat leapt straight into the air, four or five feet, and let out a wail, a screech. When it came down, it skittered off into the woods, kicking up grass and dirt. Vincent felt light-headed, dizzy. He felt panicked but didn't know why. Everything in the woods, the field, the orchard, felt off. Felt disturbed. A restlessness.

The other goats herded together and ran back through the orchard, their back ends moving up and down as they galloped away. After a few seconds, he heard a shot. His grandfather. And then a few seconds later, another shot. Still, he didn't see him. He stood against the sugar maple, hesitant to leave his post. He watched for his grandfather to emerge, dragging Thanksgiving behind him. But he never did.

Vincent found some blood, but with no snow, the goat would be difficult to track. The blood was dark, rich in color. He followed it into the woods. He stepped cautiously over downed logs, trying for some reason not to make too much noise. When he couldn't locate a body, when he lost any sign of blood, his heart quickened. His breathing grew shallow. He felt as if he were being watched.

He started making noise, rustling leaves, breaking twigs under his feet, as a way to spook the goat if it were nearby. He paced around for another minute before jogging back into the grass, the orchard. Vincent realized his grandfather was right. The goat wasn't violent. It never had any intention of charging him. It was only trying to scare him off, away from its territory. To protect itself. Vincent swelled with frustration.

He looked for his grandfather. He marched through the field at a good clip, worried about his grandfather's reaction to a wounded goat.

Vincent found him up against a tree. His rifle on the ground, his blaze orange stocking cap crooked on his head. He'd never lay his gun in the dirt unless something was the matter. His grandfather clutched his chest. His face, grimacing.

"Grandpa," he said. "Grandpa." He set his own gun on the ground next to the other. "Are you okay? What's wrong?"

"Trouble breathing," he said. "Chest pains. Nothing to worry about yet, but we do need to move."

"I heard you shoot twice," Vincent said.

His grandfather pointed to a spot twenty yards from where he stood. Vincent saw the goat, dead, tongue hanging out. His grandfather handed him a knife.

"Drag it over here," his grandfather said. "You're gonna need to field dress it."

"I've never done that," he said.

"I'm gonna teach you," his grandfather said.

It was a big female goat, smelly and dirty. Vincent dragged it back to his grandfather, who now stood on his own, arms at his sides. "Flip it on its back," his grandfather said. Vincent did as he was told; his grandfather bent over, grabbed a hoof and used his index finger to dig into the goat's fur, pushing into the base of its sternum. "Make an incision here," he said.

Vincent cut into the goat, and a deflating sound came out of it, along with a smell, so unlike anything else he would only be able to identify it as the aroma of dead goat guts. No other smell like it.

His grandfather showed him how to hold the knife so the sharp edge faced him, so he was running the knife on the inside. "The fur will dull the blade," his grandfather said. "Plus, the inside is easier to cut."

He ran the knife all the way down to the genitals. His grandfather took the knife from him, cut around the goat's anus. Then he brought the blade up and cut through its sternum, the bone and cartilage splitting. His grandfather reached into the goat, but fell back against the tree, tired and sweating. "Reach up there," he said. "Cut the esophagus and the rest of the diaphragm, then pull it down toward its groin. The guts will fall out."

"This is sick," Vincent said. He didn't mean to say it. It just happened. His grandfather hit the side of his head.

"Do it," he said. He spat on the ground. "Jesus, just do it."

He put his hands inside the goat. Warm and firm and squishy all at once. He moved his hand around the pool of blood until he felt something cord-like: the esophagus. He pulled. Nothing happened.

"Don't be a sally," his grandfather said. "Pull harder."

Everything came dangling out: heart, lungs, intestines—steam rising from the warm insides. Vincent had blood all over his hands and wrists, up to his forearms. Suddenly nauseous, he dry-heaved. His grandfather laughed. Vincent wiped his hands on a tree, smearing blood around its trunk—a maple still young enough to have smooth bark.

"Where's yours?" his grandfather said. "I heard you shoot."

With all that had just happened, he'd forgotten his wounded goat. And he knew that if he told his grandfather the truth—that he'd seen blood—they'd have to track it until they found it. Or determine that it was still alive.

"I missed," he said. His grandfather looked at him, studied his eyes. Vincent was a pretty good shot with a BB gun, always hitting the target or beer can, and he thought this was what his grandfather was thinking. But he stared back, and added, "It was running."

"Why was it running?" his grandfather said. "I'd stopped pushing them."

"It saw me move."

Still, his grandfather just looked at him. Crows were already circling above, waiting for the right moment to dive on the pile of guts. The sky was almost fully clear—mostly blue, crisp.

"Grab one of the front legs," his grandfather said, pointing at the goat. "Let's get out of here."

His grandfather lifted a hindquarter. Right away, he fell back against the tree, grimacing, grabbing at his chest.

"Actually, never mind that," his grandfather said. "Help me down. Help me to the van."

His grandfather put his arm around his shoulders. It was the first time that had happened. To Vincent the arm felt small, weak, and this surprised him. He knew his grandfather was old and out of shape, but he imagined him sturdier, stronger.

They left the goat and the guns. They descended the switchback toward the gravel road, clutching saplings and making their way.

After his grandfather was in the back of the van, lying down, he stormed back up the hill for the guns and the goat. When he got there, he looked at the pile of guts among the dirt and leaves, still steaming. He looked at his own arms, stained with blood. He looked at the goat's face. Its pupils: spooky, horizontal slits. He couldn't look at the eyes for long. Instead, he grabbed the fur around the goat's hoof. It was wet. He let the hoof drop and smelled his hands. Urine. The goat had pissed itself. He thought about the one he'd shot and wounded, wondered if it did the same thing when he hit it. Vincent grew angry again. This was his grandfather's fault. He hated him for putting them in this position, resented the fact that he'd been forced into shooting and injuring an animal. And now, having to gut and drag the one his grandfather had killed.

He wiped his face and eyes with the back of his bloodied hand. He wondered momentarily about taking his time. What if he didn't get his grandfather to the hospital? What if he stayed on the ridge? The idea tempted him. But soon—almost immediately—he was overcome with guilt. He gathered the guns under one arm and lifted the goat's leg, its hindquarters. Just before he made his way down the hill, a flock of redwing blackbirds filled the bare treetops, squawking their songs: oh-ka-lee, oh-ka-lee. From one branch to the next, they moved in no kind of pattern. Just flew. Some didn't stop at all. Some flapped overhead, just over the tops of the trees. Little black bodies peppering the clear sky. He wrenched his gaze upward until finally they'd all flown past, and there was nothing left but wooded silence. He thought of his dad's words: *The birds will tell you.* He scanned the woods in all directions, trying to find movement, trying to hear or see what might've spooked the flock. But the silence remained. And the forest remained still.

An EKG exam and stress tests. They would keep his grandfather overnight, hooked up to a monitor. Vincent could sleep on the couch. The docs told his grandfather how lucky he was. They estimated over 90 percent blockage in one of the arteries close to the heart. He'd need surgery to install a stent. But with diet change and light exercise, he'd be fine.

In the hospital room, wearing a less than sufficient gown, his grandfather told the nurses: "Hiking with my grandson." Vincent flipped pages of a *Sports Illustrated.* "He's an ambitious kid. Wanted to go on a morning hike. How can a person say no to that? Next thing I know my chest is overheating."

The nurses showed Vincent the waiting room and television. They brought him soda in a Styrofoam cup and asked him questions.

"Yeah, we were hiking south of town," he told a nurse, as it related to his grandfather's story.

"We hike all the time," he told yet another nurse.

Supporting his grandfather's made-up story felt illicit and necessary, and as he corroborated his grandfather's version of events, he felt close to him, a kind of solidarity.

"I drove him," he said, when they inquired about how they got to the hospital. This small admission seemed harmless to him, and it was. The nurses laughed. "He taught me how to drive last summer," he told them. He liked the attention. "I'll get my driver's permit as soon as I take the test."

Before coming to the hospital, they'd dropped off the goat at their house, Vincent swerving all over the roads, jerking to stops. His grandfather had yelled at him from the back of the van, "Easy does it!" But he didn't mention this to the nurses.

Next day, a nurse scheduled his grandfather's heart procedure for the following week and gave him a prescription and a flyer on heart health that suggested small amounts of exercise and foods to avoid. On the way out of the hospital, his grandfather tossed the flyer into a receptacle, tucked the prescription into his breast pocket, and said, "Time to go cut up some goat."

"You're supposed to rest," Vincent said. "That's what the doc told me."

"Docs don't know shit. I'll be fine. We'll go to the pharmacy and pick up those nitro pills in case the heart starts acting funny." His grandfather chuckled. "I'm gonna butcher the rest of that goat—show you how it's done." They'd already quartered it and stuffed it into the fridge inside the garage, next to the night crawlers and beer.

On the drive home, Vincent noticed that parts of his hands and wrists were still bloodstained. He rubbed the plum-colored smudges off his palms and fingers. He thought about what his life would be like now if he'd stayed on that ridge a little longer, left his grandfather on his own. Vincent dug hardened goat's blood out from under his nails and flicked it onto the floor as the van bumped along. He remembered the injured goat and felt a pang of guilt; he hoped he could forget about it.

But he couldn't. He thought of the goat running scared through the woods; the goat lying down and never getting back up; the goat suffering to its death. Or maybe, he hoped, it was still alive; maybe it was a surface wound; maybe the goat was still out there, roaming the hillsides and rummaging through trash and gardens. Vincent scratched his hands, harder now. His grandfather turned on the highway that led south, toward home. Vincent focused on getting his hands clean—rubbing and scratching and peeling away—trying his hardest to erase the stains from the day before.

By Sighs

This big girl comes through the door
breasts first. She barely sees what's before her:
boys, their hands bigger than dishcloths,
bigger than fly wheels, bigger than proportion.

They stumble over their own silence.
Still, the boys are full of words, stuffed with them,
every word clacking with consonants. She is
nothing but vowels, long sighs of air.

It's too much to comprehend. The boys come
and go, one moment flushed, the next bounding.
Ahh, ohh, she says, awkwardly, the sigh
wrapping itself like cellophane around her tongue.

Courtney Druz

Kingdom in Foundation

The field—it was rocks in a land of rocks, rocks pounded by the
young men and women who came to do it

to pound rocks dawn to dusk as an act of freedom, to sleep with
secret tears in the flapping tent

and the rocks became a patch of rocky dirt, sowed with scientific
passion, yielding the words of prophets, the fruit of the ground

and the fields spread, the tents solidified; the opening of hope
widened, widens, the earth spun past pinkness to bright sun—

what grew and fell there, what grew again, patches of farm and city
more commodious

farms outside the cities, crisscrossed with silver beams of water, but
only enough, the ancient measure

enough to change hands, to start a movement unfathomable,
untraceable beyond the next step, feared

the nature of it feared, given myth, given cloud, but noon could not
hold back, burning the cool mist to a hard blue

the spectrum displayed and the voice of the day singing—it is only
enough but who can grasp it, scoop it precise with fingers
beckoned in

a cast of seeds, flung out like a stone from the shore, ripples of song
as the day turns under swooping flocks

planning for the night, for the morning by extension only, only one
step conceivable, the next one

one flap of wings and the winds are shifting, the waves print subtle
ripples on the stone in space, flying on the gust of its explosion

gone and not arrived, the circle hiding a ray inside its coils, the
movement unfelt, the shape

a cell, an atom, something at the edge of vision, a thing in space,
nothing, everything.

Allison Joseph

Petition

Come rushing back to me, hasty
as a lover returned from war,
wounds ready for salve, salvation,

your ruby torrent of language
cascading like falls, delivering me
from drought, from the parched well

of a silent throat, mute mind.
Come slithering back to stroke
the resolute bones of these fingers,

make them flutter in anticipation,
in hope new phrases will tumble
onto the page, humble and humid,

seductive as sand saved from
footprints, sunwarmed and smooth.
I am the host these phrases need,

conduit for their impact,
conveyor of their import,
messenger wearied by silence,

blankness no kind of joy.
Come back to this cluttered
room, its lamp and chair,

its couch freighted by books—
bring your hymns and psalms
to dwell again among

my sinkful of dishes,
my scatterings of pencils,
my pockets full of change.

Ellen Davis Sullivan

Following Boone

It was just like Boone to come home from his tours during the worst downturn anyone could remember. Nita's son had never been particularly lucky. There was no shame in moving back into your mother's house. It seemed like everyone in Buckley had a grown child at home or lived next to someone who did. For most of Nita's life, Buckley had been the place local farmers went to get bank loans, buy tools, go to the doctor, and, if that didn't work out, get buried by the church. When she was young, Buckley was so far from the city that suburban parents brought their kids out on the weekend to go horseback riding, telling them they were going to "the country." A lot of the old-time families stuck around, giving Buckley the feel of a real town, though the malls weren't far away.

Nita didn't worry about Boone, thirty-one, not having a job. He'd done two tours in Afghanistan, and—even among vets—being out of work was common enough these days. Not much hiring going on except at the regional health center, and the only openings there—if you had no medical training—were sweeping floors and answering phones. It was hard times all around. The lawyer Nita worked for billed a lot more fees than were paid. Nita didn't have much sympathy for the delinquents. She'd paid every bill she owed, even after Russ walked out.

Nita rarely felt she had much in common with the lawyer's clients, even ones she'd grown up with. Last week, when reviewing surveillance video of a woman nearly her own age who sold a ten-dollar box of Sudafed to a meth cooker for a hundred bucks and wound up with a felony charge, Nita was stricken by the woman's bleached eyes, her stained T-shirt, her scuffed carryall—exactly like the bag Nita used for gardening tools. This put a pinprick in the disdain Nita usually felt for drug dealers. That didn't mean she wanted her son to have any truck with them. If anything, she kept after Boone even more to figure out something he could do to earn an honest living.

It had been six weeks of waiting to find out what that something would be when Nita was driving home from work one day and spotted Boone, at the curb by the courthouse, talking to a woman leaning against a Dodge Caravan. Nita jammed on the brake, transfixed by the baby Boone held: the flushed skin, scrunched knit cap, coiled fingers clutching air. She couldn't remember seeing her son cradle an infant, yet he looked like he knew what he was doing, supporting the baby's head with his long fingers. Nita didn't know what to make of the woman, though she seemed familiar. Late-thirties, Nita guessed, from the pinch of lines at her eyes and mouth.

A horn toot reminded Nita she was in the middle of the road. She glanced in the rearview and saw Officer Wylie give a "move on" wave out the patrol car window. He'd been in Boone's class in high school, but ever since his promotion, Nita had stopped calling him C.J. She was surprised he didn't come by the house any more. Married now, he probably wanted to be home with his wife and little ones, so they invited Boone over to their house. C.J. always stopped to ask Nita how she was when she saw him on the street. Just now he'd probably kept her from being rear-ended.

All the way home and into the house where she snapped on the radio, Nita kept seeing her son holding the baby with those piercing chimp eyes. If she had parked when she saw them, maybe she could have held the child too. That would have been heaven, but there was no way the woman would trust her little one to a stranger. But she wasn't a stranger. She was Boone's mother. Though how well could that girl know Boone? He never mentioned any women friends. If he was dating someone . . . . Nita's mind leapt from dating to trying to guess how old the baby was and when Boone's last leave had been. It couldn't be.

Nita longed for a grandchild. She'd given up expecting a marriage to precede the blessed event. She'd be happy if it did, of course, especially if Dinah was the bride. Her daughter seemed like she ought to be able to snag a man. She'd graduated college, worked steadily ever since—though with a lot of moving from one company to another, one coast to the other. Everyone said that's how it was these days. No one worked thirty years at the Chrysler plant in Fenton and retired with a pension any more, like Nita's father had. It wasn't even a Chrysler plant now, just a big building full of empty space.

She was picturing Dinah in a bridal gown when Boone showed up.

"I saw you out on Main Street talking to a woman with a baby. What's that about?"

"Not much."

"You know her?" Nita couldn't help asking the type of questions Boone had successfully dodged his entire life.

"Kind of."

"How can you kind of know someone?"

Boone shrugged. He had an ability to remain silent that criminals would envy.

"The baby's cute." As she said this, Nita stared at Boone, checking for any change in his face.

"Yeah," he said. "If you like that sort of thing."

At dusk Nita paged through an old album peering at her son's baby pictures. There were very few. Russ, training his trusted Canon on the backyard feeders, had been compiling a bird life list when Boone came along. The album held a complete record of Dinah's life through high school, page after page of cardinals, robins, blue jays, starlings, wrens, sparrows, and chickadees interspersed with shots of Boone's crooked-tooth smile, the early clear photos by Russ, the blurred later ones, Nita's work. She'd expected her husband to be more excited about having a boy, but like all of Russ's enthusiasms, that, too, faded quickly.

Under the single lamp Nita kept on in the evening, she tried to see a resemblance between her son and the child. Baby features were indistinct and changed fast. Look at Boone. He'd been born with slightly crossed eyes that fixed themselves over time. Russ worried their son lacked the power to focus, but Nita said he was only a baby. Nita looked again. Was there a trace of that other baby in her son's eyes? She couldn't say.

She turned up the music. Doc Watson's picking kept her from thinking about anything else, the rapid notes plucking her right out of herself. She was still staring at her son's baby picture when Boone appeared to tell her he was going out.

"Need gas money?"

"I'm riding." He pointed to the window. In the glow from the lamppost she could just make out his old ten-speed fitted with a light on the handlebars.

"Is there something I don't know?" Nita asked.

"Like what?"

"The only grown men who ride bikes around here lost their licenses from one too many DUIs."

She would never grow tired of her son's devilish laugh. "I can't spend four bucks a gallon with the mileage the truck gets."

"I hate the thought of you riding that thing in the dark. It's dangerous."

"More dangerous than South Waziristan?"

"I barely slept the whole time you were there. I told myself over and over that once you got back, I'd never worry about you again."

"Not working out like you planned?"

"Here," Nita went to her purse and pulled out her keys. "Take my car."

"What if you want to go out?"

"Where'm I going to go on a Tuesday night?"

"Sally's?"

"I see her often enough." Nita and her friend Sally had a standing date for Sundays ever since Russ moved out: lunch, or a movie, or shopping. In good weather they would sit out on the lawn wearing their straw visors and pulling weeds. Sally, who lived in the Creekside apartments, didn't care that the work benefited Nita. She said it was therapy to not think about anything but getting the next dandelion out by the root. Nita felt the same, though without Sally to talk to, she'd just as likely sit on the porch, drink iced tea, and listen to her music. It was getting harder and harder to go and do anything these days except drag herself to work, not that it was the time of year for weeding yet.

She thrust the keys at her son. They dangled from her fingers as Boone turned to go.

"I could drive you."

"I'm not fourteen." At the door, he saluted. Nita had been dismissed, or at least given all the farewell she was going to get.

She watched Boone ride off into the darkness, the shaft of his headlamp carving a narrow opening in the gloom. That light was just the kind of half-assed solution Russ would have come up with and been damned proud of it. Nita wasn't surprised Boone could find something workable. He took after his father in that way, though Boone wasn't one to thump his chest. He'd spent more time in the shed than anywhere else, so he'd know whatever was available. Nita was pretty sure that's where he and C.J. smoked when they were in high school, both the legal and illegal stuff. She hadn't wanted to know back then.

It had just been she and Boone during his high school years, with Russ gone and Dinah in college. Nita began to rely on her son for company. She made him tell her which friends he was going out with and whose house he'd be staying over at, but aside from that she let him have his space. He had chores that he mostly did and homework he didn't. Nita quit nagging him about it when it became clear Boone wasn't one for college. She knew he was smart enough to graduate high school, even if he didn't spend time with the books.

She first let up on Boone when he turned sullen, right after his father went off to Arizona during the real estate boom. Russ had fallen in with a developer he met at the Elks. As the local crop insurance agent, Russ would strike up a conversation with whoever came through town. He was someone you'd trust even though he didn't deserve it. That's how Nita ended up his wife. And why she hadn't been that surprised when he decided to go west. The developer convinced him to take on one subdivision, and if that worked out the family could move before he started on the next. At least that's what Russ told Nita.

When Russ called a few months later and put off the date for the family to join him, Dinah, a senior in high school, was happy. Nita was hurt, but not crushed. Boone had been crushed. Ever since he could walk, Boone had followed his father around every Saturday and Sunday no matter what Russ was doing, filling bird feeders, mowing the grass, talking to a neighbor about the likelihood of rain. Russ did the usual father things: went to Boone's ball games, cheered loudly, and treated Boone to pizza or ice cream after.

Still, Nita had known Russ was drifting away even before the developer told him he'd be a natural at selling houses. She'd hoped that the satisfaction of closing deals and making real money might be enough for Russ, but she hadn't been surprised when he called before Christmas to say he'd be staying out there for good and he'd send her a check each month. He'd come back once or twice, for Boone's graduation, things like that, but by then Nita could tell that her son had given up on his father, and she listened to him brag about his sales with a sense that things might not be as bright out there, in the sunshine, as Russ made it sound.

On Wednesday, Sally showed up with supper. For over a month, she'd been telling Nita they ought to go out for dinner one night a week; insisting Nita needed to eat more to keep up her strength, like she was in training. Nita said neither of them could really afford it.

"Why don't you come over to my place for supper?" Sally asked.

"I want to be around for Boone."

"There's no need for that," Sally said.

Nita didn't answer. She wasn't one to argue. Eventually her friend gave up and announced she was starting in with her own version of Meals on Wheels.

This evening Sally brought a pot of chicken stew and a pan of cornbread. She opened the refrigerator door.

"What're you doing?"

"Looking for butter for the cornbread." Crouched low, she peered past a row of ancient salad dressing, her arms twitching, as if she could barely resist the urge to throw out the crustier looking bottles. "OK, I'm going out on a limb here, but it's best not to eat eggs after the sell-by date."

"Last week you told me eggs are easy to make."

"I'm just saying."

She had to get Sally off the subject of healthy eating, a topic that could go nowhere as long as Nita felt the way she did. "I almost had an accident today. I stopped dead in the middle of Main Street when I saw Boone talking to a woman beside a van."

"That happens."

"She let him hold her baby."

"Boone?"

"I was surprised myself."

"If there's a gal who let Boone hold her baby, I-I mean . . . you don't—" Sally stood up from the fridge and bent her head back as if stooping had made her dizzy.

"You OK?"

Sally touched the side of her eye then straightened up. "I'm OK. Are you?"

Nita didn't know how to answer. At that moment, she felt good because this was the first time in so long she'd heard someone else say her son's name. No one mentioned him these days, not even her lawyers, who'd asked about him regularly when he was overseas. Maybe they'd all started to feel he should be working by now, but it had only been six weeks. As to a general answer to Sally's question, Nita had been feeling poorly. Sally would say it was not eating, but Nita knew it was worse than that.

"How's Gwen doing?" Nita usually avoided asking about Sally's daughter. She suspected the girl, who'd never done anyone a good turn in her life, would show up at the office one day, needing a lawyer for some thing or other.

"She got laid off from Burger King. She said the manager kept cutting her hours until it didn't make sense for her to get cleaned up and go to work."

"That's a shame." Nita knew she shouldn't let it, but pride in her children swelled in her heart when she compared them to Sally's daughter, a girl who couldn't keep a fast food job. She also knew that, having asked about Gwen, Sally would be forced to ask about Dinah, and she did. "Oh, you know, she's flying around the country on those real estate deals she does. I can't keep track of all of it."

"She still has to do that? Even after she got promoted?"

"I think she enjoys it, going from place to place."

"Sure doesn't take after you."

Everyone knew Nita was scared of flying. She'd never gone out to Seattle to visit Dinah. She wasn't able to overcome her fear, despite her daughter's pleading. "You'd love it out here," Dinah would say. Nita didn't disagree. She didn't go either.

After the meal, Sally insisted Nita keep the rest of the food; in exchange, Nita insisted Sally not help with the dishes. "I don't want to leave you with this mess," Sally said.

"It'll give me something to do until Boone gets home."

"You've got to stop waiting around for him."

"Don't you have Gwen living with you?"

"That's different. She'd get her own place if she could afford it."

Nita hadn't meant to push so hard, but she was weary of Sally's advice. The pot and the kettle, her mother would have called them.

At the door, Sally turned back. "Don't let that stew go to waste." Nita promised not to, though if she were young, she would have crossed her fingers behind her back as she said it.

The voices didn't start until Nita was alone, in her yellow gloves, sponging the counter. Or maybe they started sooner, but it was only then that they grew loud enough for her to hear them over the radio.

"I said I would." Her son's voice, deeper than Nita had realized, a man's rumble that didn't have to be stirred up to resonate.

"I'm just saying you don't know what all's involved." The woman sounded more disappointed than angry. Or maybe that was what Nita wanted to believe, that Boone wouldn't hurt anyone on purpose; but being his father's son, he couldn't help but let a woman down now and then.

"I said I would."

"Then why'd it take me coming here for you to decide?"

Nita shut off the radio. It had to be the woman with the baby. Nita wanted to see the little one again, but by the time she reached the front room, they were gone. There was no Caravan parked out front, no car at all by the curb. Boone must have gone with them, though Nita hadn't heard the front door close, either coming or going.

During the night, Nita got up. She didn't put on a light. She'd hardly slept in more than a month. It made her shaky, barely able to focus on the documents she had to read at work. Dinah told her to go to the doctor, who could prescribe something, but Nita was afraid of becoming dependent.

"You'll only take them as long as you need to get over this," her daughter said.

"I'm not trying to get over anything."

"That's exactly why you should go."

Nita didn't listen. Dinah was from a generation that didn't understand how dangerous drugs could be. Nita saw that every day at the office. Instead, she kept the house as dark as possible at night and let herself get out of bed if she tossed around for too long. She could tell right away Boone wasn't home. It wasn't that she couldn't hear the rustle of his breathing. That was more imagined than real, since he always slept with his bedroom door closed. Nita could feel the absence of another body in the house. It's what kept her from sleeping after Boone shipped out. She worried. What if she suddenly had one of those silent heart attacks she'd read about in *Prevention*? It was just like nature to give women fatal illnesses that don't come with obvious signs like the squeezing chest pains men get. Awake and worried, Nita would lie in bed picturing Boone with a burlap sack over his head, seated cross-legged on the floor in front of a turbaned man holding a machine gun. Her breath would come fast and she'd feel sure the thud of her heartbeat was something more than the result of a mother's effort to stretch her arms six-thousand-miles across the ocean.

Nita made her way down the dim hall. She pushed open her son's bedroom door. A ray of moonlight crept through the hopsack drapes. Bed neatly made, video game boxes lined up in a row, no Boone. The bed was so tightly cornered, it looked as if it hadn't been touched in weeks. Nita reached for the bureau to steady herself. That was just military style. She closed the door.

She didn't bother getting back into bed. There was no way she'd fall into a real sleep now. In the light of the gas burner, she made a cup of herbal tea. She sat in the rocker in the living room facing the picture window. There was a glimmer of light outside when she heard the paper boy on his bicycle, the squeal of tires ridden too fast. She pictured the rolled newsprint arcing through the air. She didn't get up to bring it in. If there were a story of a big car crash, bodies taken to the hospital or worse, she'd wait to find out.

She must have slipped into a light sleep, the kind that doesn't produce any rest, because she started when the sun speckled her eyes. She stood, stiff from the chair, but not much worse than she was most mornings with the pain in her knees. She'd avoided the extra pounds other women her age had added over the years, but nothing could keep arthritis from getting you if you were old enough. She needed to get ready for work. On her way to shower, she peered into Boone's room. He still hadn't come home.

That evening, when she got back from work, Boone must have been puttering out in the shed. Nita didn't call him for dinner. She couldn't start questioning him about where he'd been all last night. He was a grown man. Besides, he'd say he wasn't hungry, that he'd stopped for pizza. He never said what Nita knew to be true, that her dinners weren't worth coming inside for these days—some warmed up bean soup, a couple pieces of toast. She could have offered Sally's leftovers, but he'd never been one for chicken stew.

She looked through the kitchen window just as Boone was striking out again on his bicycle, another ride into the dusk. This time she was determined to find out where he was going. It had to have something to do with that woman with the baby, but since Nita didn't know her name or address, her only hope was to follow Boone. She ran to the car and was grateful it started right up, Hazel Dickens on the radio singing "A Few Old Memories."

Nita caught a glimpse of her son pedaling along about a block ahead. She accelerated slowly, staying far enough back that Boone couldn't be sure it was her, should he turn around. Of course he wasn't likely to swivel his head a full one-eighty. He didn't have those little mirrors she'd seen once or twice attached to the eyeglasses of guys riding bikes. Why would she think of those? Boone didn't even wear glasses.

At the first light on Main Street, Boone sped up. The light turned yellow, and Nita would have been stuck at the red, losing sight of him, so she pushed the pedal hard. She hadn't gone more than a block when a police car pulled alongside, forcing her to slow down, then stop. C.J. leaned across the front seat of the patrol car. She lowered her window and shut off the radio.

"Mrs. H."

"Officer Wylie."

"What're you doing out here?"

"I'm following Boone."

"What?" C.J. looked away. "Oh."

It was growing increasingly dim as the last of the sun's rays withered. The streetlights ended just past the fire station.

"Where do you think he could go?" the police officer asked.

"If I knew I wouldn't have to follow him."

C.J. hesitated as if he couldn't puncture this bit of logic. Or maybe he had something else on his mind. "I think you know where Boone is, Mrs. H."

"No, see, the woman with the baby came by the other evening, and she was trying to convince Boone of something, but I couldn't—"

As she said this, Nita could tell it sounded wrong. She couldn't believe she'd let it go this far. Making a fool of herself in front of C.J.

"I think it'd be best for you to follow me back to your place." He pulled in front of her.

Nita knew it'd be hopeless to keep going. The patrol car started up, and she couldn't see what to do except follow. She concentrated on the red taillights, the blinker as C.J. turned right and right and right, then left, putting them back on Main Street going the other way. She drove in silence, as if she were pulling weeds or checking off items on an evidence list. With her faculties engaged in that loose way, she remembered where she'd first seen the woman with the baby. That was the trouble with doing rote tasks, all alone, no music playing. Thoughts came unbidden, piercing the dense clay that filled Nita's head.

It had been the day of the funeral. At the cemetery, Nita was standing alongside the hole in the ground when the van pulled up. She wasn't one to pay much attention to cars, and normally she wouldn't know what kind it was, but when the door slid back, a low whine started up. A man wearing a uniform was inching lower to the ground in a wheelchair. Nita couldn't bear how he tried to look like he had nothing to do with this noise that stifled all conversation, so she stared at the letters on the back of the car. The woman came around and settled a black-eyed baby into the man's inert lap. After the service, she pushed the man in the chair over to Nita. He introduced himself and shook her hand with his rubberized fingers. The baby gazed up at her. Nita fixed on the child.

"Your son was a true hero," the man said. "He had a split-second to make a decision at that checkpoint and he did the right thing. Saved a lot of lives, and you've got the medals to prove it."

Nita didn't want medals. She didn't want proof. There was only one thing she wanted. She punched the radio button and swerved onto the first side street. Knowing Boone wouldn't be there, she couldn't go home. The patrol car's brake lights pulsed red, but C.J. didn't swing around to chase after her. It wasn't a major crime to run a traffic light, only a Class C misdemeanor. Nita was clear on that much. The other clear thing she could hear, like a song on the radio, was Sally saying: "Come over anytime." Nita had never dropped in on someone after dark. She hoped it wasn't too late.

Danielle LaVaque-Manty

Down the Hatch

Hot chocolate. Root beer. Kool-Aid.

This minty chemical foam they used to call a "Shamrock Shake." My mother must have thought there was real ice cream in there.

Crazy amounts of coffee. The year I worked as a barista? Holy crap.

Champagne on our first date. You were so cute trying to pop the cork.

Pepto-Bismol before every big pitch to a client.

Champagne at our wedding. Better and more. That was one expensive hangover.

Red Bull every night for a month during the campaign for the big kahuna.

Vodka tonics when the big kahuna cut bait. You drank more of them than I did.

Gallons of chamomile after you told me about your affair.

Nyquil to sleep after you left.

Everclear when I heard you were going to marry that slut.

Kefir for the ulcer after they downsized me.

Prune juice for that other problem.

Kale smoothies. Kale smoothies. Kale smoothies.

Battery acid.

Kidding. I'm saving that for a special occasion.

Stop by for a drink any time.

Catherine A. Brereton

Between *Change* and *Rain*

She tells me that she's told me this before, but I'm certain that she hasn't.

"We were all taken to the convent," she explains, pausing to raise a mug to her lips and sip at her tea. I'm looking in her direction, but can't bring myself to look at her face. My eyes settle on a graying chip in the mug. It's her favorite mug; that's why she still uses it, even though it's been battered from too many encounters with the sink. I bought it for her for Mother's Day one year, although I've forgotten exactly which year. It has bright red chickens painted on a white background. She loves chickens.

I cradle my own mug of tea with both hands intently, watching three bubbles gather and pop on the top of the tan liquid.

"Your granddad—well, he just couldn't look after us after Mam left," she says, between sips, her Irish accent thick around the liquid. "He liked his drink too much, and they decided we weren't safe with him, so they took us and put us in the convent. Me, Sadie, Kathleen, Anne, and Helen. Our Hugh came too, but him and Helen were only wee babbies so they went to the nursery."

I can't think of a single response that feels safe, so I look farther away from her face, over her shoulder at a brass clock on the wall. Next to it, a matching barometer, resting between *change* and *rain*. Dad walks past, taps the barometer three times with the tip of his index finger, and the filigree hand wobbles a millimeter closer to rain. He grunts with annoyance. He always hopes it's broken, always hopes that the filigree hand will remain still, always disappointed by the result. Somehow, a broken barometer would be a better option than the prediction of yet another overcast sky, heavy and dark, outside the kitchen window. There's a click, and a bulb hanging from the kitchen ceiling casts its yellow light around the room, blanketing us in strange shadows.

"You've never told me this before," I say.

In a pushchair in the corner of the room, my sleeping one-year-old stirs in her sleep, blinking her long-lashed eyes at the dim world. Mum scrapes her chair back on the quarry-tiled floor.

"Ach, I have. You've just never listened."

She tells me that she has a book for me to read. Sixteen years have passed, my sleepy one-year-old is now old enough to drive, and the scuffed table occupies a different kitchen in a different house. I'm sitting on her couch, visiting home for three weeks while I take care of government paperwork that will take me away from her forever. Dad lifts his head from his magazine.

"Which one?"

"*Suffer the Little Children.*" She tips her head forwards slightly as she speaks. I know without asking what the book is about, but I'm a coward and say nothing. Dad puts down his magazine and turns on the television.

She will cry when she drops me off at the airport in three weeks time; neither of us will have mentioned the book again.

She tells me, finally, what really happened. We've discovered that our relationship holds up better with distance, although 4,000 miles seems excessive. Very occasionally now, we Skype, but I don't want to see her face on the day I decide to ask her about Nazareth House. I'd rather not know if it makes her cry. I'd rather keep my guilt about not knowing away from her scrutiny. In the midst of a Facebook chat, I ask her about the book. I've tracked down a copy on Amazon, but it's selling for almost $200. I ask her if she'd be willing to buy a copy over in England and send it to me. It's time, I tell her, that I filled in the blanks. As it happens, I tracked down the wrong book, and she points me in the right direction to a much less expensive volume. I "click to buy" and the story of her childhood is on its way to me for just under $4, including shipping. There's something about that price, but I refuse to reflect on it.

She replies with a colon and an end parenthesis when I tell her I've bought the book. The chat box tells me she's still typing, but I'm congenitally impatient so I click to another screen, run quick fingers over the keyboard, and flick through the options helpfully provided by Google. There's a newspaper report, an account of the "sadistic treatment" a girl called Frances Reilly endured "at the hands of the nuns"[i] charged with taking care of her. She was bathed in Jeyes Fluid, locked in a cupboard, and used as a human mop to clean up her own urine. My nostrils fill with the remembered smell of Jeyes Fluid—we used it to disinfect dog kennels. I imagine it on my skin, and I blanche. When I click back to our Facebook chat, Mum has typed that Frances Reilly had contacted her a couple of years previously.

Did you know her before then?

Yes, I was in Nazareth House at the same time as her.

It takes me a moment to process this.

How old were you?

I was seven when we went.

How old were you when you left?

Fifteen.

I don't know what Mum looked like as a seven-year-old; to the best of my knowledge, there are no photographs of her from the Nazareth House years, and certainly none from the years before that. She tells me that there are a couple of pictures in Frances Reilly's book, and she thinks that a couple of her sisters are in them, but not her. She doesn't remember much about it, she says. She doesn't remember any of the things that Frances Reilly talks about, but couldn't tell me why. I don't push her.

Though I don't know what she looked like as a seven-year-old, I know exactly what she looks like now. I know exactly where she's sitting too—in the high-backed chair next to the front room window. There's a table next to her, and she'll have the laptop perched on a tray on her knees. She'll have a mug of tea at her side. The mug with the chickens has long since been broken beyond repair; when I saw her over the summer she was using a china mug decorated with geese. The inside of the mug is stained with the residue from a thousand teabags. I scrubbed it clean when I was there last, but I'm pretty sure the staining will have built up again.

I don't remember a lot of the things. Maybe that's because I was one of the cleverer ones. It was still tough though.

I'm sorry I haven't made time to talk to you about this before.

She doesn't answer me immediately.

People don't know the half of it. Frances wanted me to help her but I don't have enough firm memories. Besides, it's all in the past now.

Just a stain in a china mug, I think.

A couple of days later, an email from Amazon informs me that *Suffer the Little Children* is "out for delivery." Prompted to remember the conversation I'd been trying to forget, I search the Internet for details of Nazareth House, expecting nothing and finding too much. By sheer coincidence, The Historical Institutional Abuse Inquiry had started just a few days ago. The sleek navy and white website quietly announced the largest child abuse inquiry ever held in the United Kingdom,[ii] investigating claims of abuse spanning over seventy years, from 1922 to 1995.[iii] Mum was left at Nazareth House in 1959. She tells me that she spent a year before that in another orphanage. Gleneyre was okay, she says, but they couldn't keep the siblings together as they grew up, so, one by one, they were sent to Nazareth House.

Once an imposing red brick building with narrow windows and turrets from something more befitting a gothic drama, Nazareth House has been demolished. In its place stands a private, modern "care village" with every possible amenity for Belfast's aging (and affluent) citizens. Ironically, one of the nuns alleged to have taken part in the abuse is now a resident—or so the investigation records tell me. I peer at the glossy images. There's no trace of the high wall that enclosed the grounds, no sign of the arched black door through which the children passed, and the high trees that screened the house from the outside world have long since been chopped down. Nazareth House is determined to fade without a trace, and until now, I've been willing to let it.

The book arrives in an innocuous padded envelope, complete with a handwritten note from the seller, asking me if I'll leave positive feedback for the prompt delivery of my mother's past. It feels surprisingly light for a hardback. Cheap paper. I set it aside, push it into a corner on the kitchen table, put other books on top of it—a few bills that need to be paid, an empty mug, an overripe banana that needs to be thrown away. There it waits. I see the spine when I enter the kitchen each morning, so I rearrange the pile and throw away the banana that has begun to smell vaguely alcoholic. I move the mug, eventually, pay the bills, drag a different book out of the pile, replace that book with a library book that needs to be returned. I fill the empty space left by the mug with a water bottle and an unopened box of herbal teabags purchased as a gift for a friend. There's a discarded scarf over a nearby chair; a silk tassel drapes conveniently in front of the still-exposed spine. Jeoffrey, my one-eared cat, jumps onto the back of the chair, knocks the scarf onto the floor, topples over the water bottle, and dislodges the carefully stacked pile of books. The whole shebang concertinas across the table. There's a bill I forgot to pay, a school form I should have completed weeks ago, and, of course, the book.

I start to read it that night.

I am critical, for this book is not well written.

Each page is an effort of will; each word sits heavily on the cheap paper. I'm convinced that when I turn the page, the words will fall through the thin leaves and tumble to the floor, where they can be swept up and thrown away. I muscle my way through, searching for a mention of a name I'll recognize. I skip to the glossy pages of photographs in the middle. I see someone who looks like my Aunt Helen, but I can't tell. No one looks like my mum. I move back to the narrative, unmoved. As awful as this story is—and it *is* awful—I cannot connect. My lack of response takes me by surprise. I am known in our family for having hyperactive tear ducts—even a half emotion is expressed in salt water form—yet now I show nothing. I flick through the pages, annoyed, waiting for something to strike me. Only boredom and distaste. And maybe anger.

I slide the book onto the shelf of my bedside table, and pile a few more books on top of it, a bottle of body lotion, a box of tissues. It is low enough to the floor that I cannot see the edge of the pages unless I am bending down looking for it. I begin to avoid vacuuming that part of the room. Dislodged hair and dust gather in tiny clumps beneath the table. I don't use the body lotion or the tissues, and I forget which books are now excluded from my library, sent to Coventry. I clear my Internet browser history, forget the name of the investigation, and, when Mum's birthday rolls around, I decide to Skype her. I want to see her face.

She tells me that she loves me before we disconnect. Her webcam reveals an antimacassar over the back of her chair, a heavy tapestry decorated with hunting scenes. A door opens in the corner of the room; Dad walks past, then disappears from view. I hear the metal latch of a different door closing. I make small talk with Mum about the weather, the dogs, my brothers. She asks me to knit her a hat to match the scarf I sent for her birthday, and I promise I will. The door latch clinks again and a mug is thrust in front of the screen. There are the familiar geese and a new, white chip on the rim. She raises the mug to her lips. The television booms to life from another corner, the volume cranked as high as it will go, and she can no longer hear me.

"I'd better go, Cath. Your dad's program is on in a minute."

I promise, again, to make the hat and that I'll Skype in a couple of weeks. There's a pause.

"I love you, Mum."

Her hand wavers over the keyboard. She looks away from the screen, across at the television.

"I love you too."

She has barely uttered the last word before the screen goes blank.

[i] Reilly, Frances. "Abuse motion goes some way to righting wrongs." *Belfast Telegraph*. 2nd November 2009. Accessed online 5th September 2014. http://www.belfasttelegraph.co.uk/opinion/abuse-motion-goes-some-way-to-righting-wrongs-28501442.html

[ii] http://www.hiainquiry.org/

[iii] "Historical Institutional Abuse inquiry: the background." *BBC News Northern Ireland*. 13th January 2014. Accessed online 5th September 2014. http://www.bbc.co.uk/news/uk-northern-ireland-25637486

Timothy Duffy

Name

She tells me over coffee that her son had my name.
We aren't together, but our proximity is enough.
When my name is said aloud, it is already an invitation.
Had my name—called him every variation,
Tim for adulthood and tween swagger.
Timmy for tender moments:
privileged use by the infirm and female.
Timothy for full Greek weight.
Timere
Timeo—I have come to fear, to seek
whichever gods are trusted with the names of those
who no longer own what they are called.

What receptacle am I for such ephemera?
I am *he* I want to say
What more is in this name?
I am he—I have never been anyone else.
Where else do names go if not within
a trembling epitaph always suddenly nearby?
Some stranger with a familiar flag, thinking:
I know I can't be the first of what I am.
and:
I can be yours, if just for now. Silently.

Before the Morning After

The revolution
will not be subsidized
by the government
you're trying to depose.

Father why would I
follow you into the streets
to stand among the men
and women who vote

against their self-interest?
I know you only want to extend
your influence. Is it not enough
that I love you against

my better judgement?
Did you ever wonder
what your designer clothes
might say about your views

on inequality?
Believe me I get the joke,
when you call us all for burgers
to discuss "What's next?"

and I'm sitting here
in national dress, next to
protestors and policemen,
asking for more mustard.

Surely diet and a bit of exercise
are on that list?

Kyle Ensrude

Dead She Said

"Dead," she said.

I walked over to the rocky beach and bent my knees to examine it.

"I think it's a pike." A slimy, pale fish about the length of a ruler lay there dead, washed up on shore.

"Ahead of his time, but at least he tried," she said.

"Couldn't wait for legs to sprout?"

The sun was setting over the pines surrounding Lake Mariah. They were tall and narrow, slender sentries guarding a hidden pool. We had been walking the trails, mostly silent, for an hour or two. It was one of those especially warm October days, when the world seems that much more beautiful because you know fall will come soon; the leaves will drop and the sun will slowly retreat. But for the moment— at least for one more day—our bare arms still felt warm in the sunlight that shone through the canopy, and the trees were all painted with the rich palette of autumn.

"Think he was bored?" I said, still hunched over and gazing at the dead fish.

"Bored?"

"Maybe he thought he could have more fun somewhere else," I said.

"The fish?"

"Maybe he did…"

"Maybe," she said. "Maybe he just felt that dying on the shore was preferable to living in a lake he didn't like."

"I like this lake."

"It's kind of small."

"That's why I like it."

"You can't even tube on it."

"Fuck tubing. I'd rather paddle a canoe."

Still bent low, I picked up a small twig that was caught between the tide and the tall grass. Grasping it between my thumb and index finger, I moved it toward the fish slowly, like it was a scalpel and I was a surgeon about to make an incision. The tip of my tongue hung out the side of my mouth like it always did when I was concentrating. I stopped just before my scalpel reached the scales, took a deep breath, and, with a sudden flick of my wrist, nudged the stick into the side of the fish. Its tail twitched with a weak slap and its gills gasped for water.

"Jesus," I said. "He's still alive."

"What time is sundown?" she asked.

"Should I help him back into the water?"

"I want to leave before it gets too late," she said.

"He's pretty far gone. Maybe it's best to let him die in peace."

"I'm just tired," she said.

"It won't be long now—sun's almost down." She sighed behind me.

"Who cares about the fish?"

I stood and looked over my shoulder. "What do you mean?"

She approached the shore and stood beside me, glaring down at the fish. She glanced and saw I was still considering it. Without warning, she kicked the fish as hard as she could and sent it flying into the tall grass beside the lake.

"It's dead," she said, and walked away. I could hear the grass rustle as the fish thrashed desperately in one last exhausted attempt to survive. She was already back on the trail, distancing herself from me.

"I know the feeling," I said, alone, and walked back to the trail. Catching up to her, I spoke from behind. "You didn't have to do that."

"Do what?"

"You didn't have to kick him like that." I said.

"You'd still be hunched over it like an idiot if I hadn't."

"So what? You didn't have to kick him."

"Maybe we should have just put him out of his misery."

I fell silent and shuffled along behind her. I didn't care about the leaves above me anymore; in the diminishing light, the red and yellow hues turned brown. I bent my neck and looked at my feet; it suddenly occurred to me how strange they looked. I was wearing old white sneakers, stained and muddied from the trails. I suddenly became very self-conscious of my feet, acutely aware of their presence. They propelled me forward without any direction. These two tired, aching feet inside these old, muddy sneakers kept pushing through the dirt with the assumption that the rest of my body knew where it was going. I was so hyperaware of my feet that I became conscious of the way every muscle moved over cartilage and bone, and I started to feel each nerve ending firing like a million little cannons attached to the same fuse. The feeling became so intense and uncomfortable that I started trying to communicate to my feet the proper way to walk, like trying to tell your lungs how to breathe when hyperventilating. I started to stumble over myself, bringing down first my toe, then my heel, and almost falling over into the dirt.

"What's wrong with you?" she asked.

I sat down on a log just off the trail.

"I can't keep going," I said. I leaned back to take the weight off my feet.

"Come on, we're almost done."

"I can't," I said.

"But we're right at the end."

I tipped my head back and closed my eyes to the darkening sky.

"Why'd you have to kick him?" I said. "Why couldn't you just leave him be?"

"I want to leave."

"Why can't you ever just look at something?"

"Because it was ugly... I want to leave."

"Maybe if you really looked at it, you wouldn't mind that it was ugly. You never see the beauty in ugly things."

"It's over. You need to forget about it. You can never let things go."

"I can let go. I just can't kick things away like that."

"You can never let go, just like—"

"Like what?"

"Forget it. If this is how you want to end things, then so be it. I didn't have to come anyway; I only did it out of courtesy."

"Some courtesy."

"I'm leaving." She turned around and began to walk away. "You better hurry up if you expect to get a ride."

"I'm through chasing after you," I said. I watched her walk away until she was out of sight. I found myself in darkness; the sun had gone down and the moon was nowhere to be found. It was just my luck to choose tonight, of all nights, to lose myself in the woods.

After a few minutes of self-pity, I stood up. The night was black and I could see little in front of me. It was strangely quiet that night, save for the faint lapping of the lake against the shore. The lapping of the waves was the only sure thing I knew, the only real direction I could take, so I began to stumble my way back toward the sound of the water. It became louder and louder—I was getting close. Although it was dark and my feet barely worked, I somehow managed to reach the lake without falling.

I found myself standing in the tall grass that hugged the edge of the water. It was soft and cool, so with nothing else to do I lay down and rested my head on the wet earth. My eyes became heavy as I heard a cricket begin to chirp on the far side of the lake, a comforting tune like a lullaby. Before long, I fell asleep.

When I finally awoke it felt like I had slept for a thousand years, but it must have been only a few hours. The moon had risen, shining like a jewel. The single cricket that had lulled me to sleep still sang but was joined by thousands of others, chirping in the night. The soft lullaby had become a symphony rising to crescendo. The sleep and the music rejuvenated my body and my soul; I felt triumphant. The tall grass towered above me, but I could see the moon shining through the blades. I decided to go for a swim. I began to slap my tail and wriggle my body in the grass, inching ever closer to the lake. The rustle of the dewy grass sounded like a crowd cheering me on; the song of the crickets was my anthem. With one final thrust, I flopped my body and vaulted out of the grass and into the air, landing gracefully in the water's cool embrace.

Fabiyas M V

Bharatanatyam Dancer

Kanisha's head, fingers, and remaining toes move instinctively and rhythmically as she watches the *bharatanatyam*, a classical Indian dance, performed by her friend Nayana in the school auditorium. There are ten contestants in the *bharatanatyam* dance category. The noisy students have conquered all the benches and chairs in front of the stage. Kanisha sits in the last row, her crutches and frustration resting nearby.

The seed of dance had sprouted in Kanisha's soul: she couldn't oppress her obsession to learn the *bharatanatyam*.

"My classmate Nayana's joined a dance class. Ma, I also want to learn the *bharatanatyam*." She opened her heart in front of her mother, who was sitting like a crow-pheasant in a broken cane chair.

"We can't even think of that, my dear. It's very expensive."

"Ma . . . Ma, please . . . please." She insisted.

Paru was chewing a betel leaf, along with tiny pieces of areca nut. Like the other parents in her village, Paru wished to bring her child into the limelight. But can a squirrel open its mouth the same way an elephant can?

Paru dipped in the canal and picked up the black oysters from the muddy bottom. She brought the oysters home in a bamboo basket, scooped the flesh, and boiled it. The rustics would buy the oyster flesh from her. Sometimes, she earned her livelihood by catching tiny prawns with a small, sieve-like net. She would dry the prawns in the parching sunlight, then walk door-to-door, selling them.

Paru didn't like her daughter falling into sloth. She decided to find an additional income to pay the dance fee, no matter how inconvenient. She took her daughter to Sarigama Dance School.

Roshini, the dance teacher, got up from her fiber chair and showed Kanisha a *mudra*, signing with her fingers, then asked Kanisha to repeat the steps. She did it amazingly well. Next, the teacher displayed a charming facial expression, which Kanisha also imitated.

"There's a spark in your daughter. It's really marvelous!" The teacher took an interest in her new pupil. Before leaving, Paru did not forget to draw a verbal portrait of her penury for the dance teacher to note.

Kanisha went zealously to Sarigama Dance School in Chava City. Her classmate, Nayana, was a dance student there, as well. The school was adjacent to Roshini's house.

It's a serious dance form. "We take an event from *Mahabharata*, our epic," Roshini told her, explaining the utter importance of the dance. We present it through our facial expressions, graceful style, gross bodily movements, acting, devotion . . . " And Kanisha was all ears.

Kanisha manipulated her body gracefully, completely in tune with the music of the dance. Pain and pleasure appeared on her face in turn.

"Ma, please come. Watch me dance."

Kanisha invited her mother on a Sunday night. She had completed one year of training under Roshini.

"No. Not now. I'm very busy. I've so much work to do in the kitchen."

"You can do that later, Ma."

Paru couldn't resist her daughter's tenacity.

A lone bulb, hanging from a bamboo pole buttressing the roof, shed dim light. Moths swarmed the bulb—there was a drizzle outside, forcing them in. Paru watched her daughter transform into a wonderful dancer; rapture filled in her heart. "Excellent!" She clapped and embraced her daughter.

"Ma, I'm sure I'll win first place in the next school youth festival." Unbound joy echoed within the walls of their home; it was a small hut, built with financial assistance from the Panchayat.

"You're now fit for the debut," Roshini told her.

Kanisha's face lit up with pride and pleasure at hearing her teacher's words. She carried that message of pride and pleasure to her mother.

"Ma . . . fix . . . fix the day for my debut . . ." She was panting.

They went to Roshini's house. In a pious setting, as per the codes of custom, Kanisha presented Roshini with *Guru Dhakshina*, a violet silk sari adorned with white blooms, and a cash gift of five thousand rupees. She touched the feet of her "guru." The teacher was very grateful and blessed her pupil, placing her palms upon her head. They reached a decision about the day for the debut: it would be on the day of their temple festival, next Saturday. Nayana's debut would be on the same day, the teacher mentioned.

When she returned home from school in the afternoon, Kanisha found her mother putting the dance costumes, coloring powder, anklets, and so forth, into the bag, which they'd received as a gift from Sanora Silks, a readymade shop at Chava.

"Come on, dear. I'm packing for tomorrow. See if anything's missing."

"Okay, Ma. Tomorrow's the day. I can't even imagine it." There was an amalgam of joy and tension in her mother's countenance. Paru had borrowed a lot of money from her rich neighbors to buy the expensive costume of the *bharatanatyam*. She didn't know how to repay it.

Her neighbor's auto rickshaw, which Paru had already arranged, came by at 7:00 p.m. Kanisha stood before her father's photograph hanging on a nail in the wall: she bowed her head, brought her palms together, and silently sought his blessings. Her coolie father died of a viper bite a decade ago, when she was just four years old. They set off at 7:10 p.m.

A big lamp opened its eye beside the banyan tree in the temple yard. There was an open stage under the tree.

8:00 p.m.

At first, it was Nayana's debut. Her schoolmate danced in the limelight on the stage. But the *bharatanatyam* lovers were not contented with Nayana's performance.

8:30 p.m.

Kanisha walked to the stage like a peacock, feeling the weight of many eyes falling upon her body. She stood like a bloomed blossom on the stage. A song describing an event in *Mahabharata* flowed through the mike. She drew a beautiful saga in the air with her fingers. Her entire body moved in perfect rhythm. Diverse patterns of emotions flashed on her face. The spectators tapped their fingers rhythmically on their thighs and nodded their heads in unison with the dance and the music. She really dazzled the spectators with her top-notch performance. "Fantastic!" Her mother whispered, everybody whispered. Her performance was far better than that of her friend, Nayana. Even Nayana may have known this.

9:30 p.m.

They started their journey home by the same auto rickshaw. Paru was very proud of her daughter. Pride, transiently, let her forget her penury. There were ripples of pleasure in Kanisha's mind. The auto rickshaw moved like a tortoise. Quite unexpectedly, a stray dog, a white one with black spots all over its body, attempted to cross the road. The driver essayed to stop the vehicle immediately, to save the dog: *alas!* a jeep, running just behind, crashed into the back of the auto rickshaw with a thunderous sound. People approached from the darkness and gathered around the rickshaw, which rested upside down on the roadside. Three of them were taken to the hospital.

"The girl's condition is worst," a street vendor observed.

Paru's and the driver's wounds were not deep. But Kanisha had to spend nearly a month in the ICU of the Alpha Hospital. The jeep struck the side where she was sitting—her right leg was trapped under the wheel. The doctor was forced to remove her damaged right leg—and her dreams along with it.

Now the waves of an announcement echo in the school auditorium. "Dear teachers and students, here's the result of the *bharatanatyam* contest, HS section. First place goes to Nayana . . ."

Nayana, in her dance dress, walks to the stage like a princess to receive the certificate; her pride flashes in and out; the cameras gobble her glittering body: a precious moment of luck borne out of a tragic fate. Innocent Kanisha stands up on her crutches to honor the winner and hides her broken heart beneath a charming smile.

Stacey Balkun

The domestic mermaid is a rose

a hydrangea, delicate blue blossom.
She hates roses and she hates hydrangeas most.
For her birthday, the domestic mermaid's husband gave her a
compass

on a gold chain. It gets caught in the carpet
when she tidies up, says north is one way in mornings
and in evenings, the needle flips around.

When she said she missed the ocean, he bought
a waterbed and then a betafish
but it didn't speak her language.

She lined the windowsills with seashells
but he broke them up above the flower bed,
said calcium would be good for the soil.

She chain-smokes in the bathtub
drinking a bottle of Fisheye chardonnay
that her husband had tried to hide

but she found it so she drinks it empty
then slips a letter into the bottle—
an SOS disguised as a love poem.

She wants to like the cat
but he always nips at her tail.
When her husband comes home from work

with French bread and fried oysters—an
offering—she hopes he won't smell
the alcohol on her breath. Eats everything on her plate.

The Beauty in a Storm

We finger painted the sky last night—
asphalt smeared palms splattered discord,
creating a storm above the silent suburb.
Dried blood from our bitten nails
gave the clouds a sinister smile.

The shingling of the roof inked patterns on our backs,
the freckles in our eyes danced with delight while
our paintbrush fingers stole words from our tongues.
Each careless flick of our wrists a new note
in the dissonant song of the storm.

Our nails chipped away at this chaos
unveiling a light so pure it put the stars to shame.
The sky cried with envy while I cried to you;
I would never be that beautiful—
I wonder if the sky felt that way, too.

A sigh escaped your granite-lined lips
as your whispers molded the makings of my brain.
"You are not beautiful, and neither am I.
But look what we've done here, love.
We've made a mess of the sky."

Erin Kaempf
CONTRIBUTING EDITOR

How We Write About Our Lives:
An Exploration in Books

In an article published earlier this year in *The New York Times Magazine*, Karl Ove Knausgaard describes an uneventful trip into the American heartland with exhilarating, hypnotic force. That he is able to turn a series of mishaps and thwarted plans into a riveting travel essay comes as no surprise to those who have read his six-novel series *My Struggle*. Among the many admirers of this series is the beloved American author Jeffrey Eugenides, who remarks on Knausgaard's fourth and most recent novel available in English: "How wonderful it is to read an experimental novel that fires every nerve ending while summoning in the reader the sheer sense of how amazing it is to be alive, on this planet and no other."

The experimental nature of *My Struggle* is not overwrought invention, but an adherence to the prosaic moments that make up a life. The narrator's reality is Knausgaard's reality, from boyhood through adulthood, albeit slightly transformed: names are changed and certain liberties are taken to round out memories—recalling a teenage night of debauchery, for example, proves challenging years after the fact. There is a quiet, overwhelming thrill while reading *My Struggle*. Having been invited into an author's life by way of a thinly veiled novel, the reader has opportunity to engage in a private voyeurism—to transgress on intimate ground with the permission of the subject. What makes this work such a tour de force for Eugenides also compels him to remark that Knausgaard traverses a fine line between fabrication and remembrance: "But the selection process he subjects his memories to in order to fulfill the narrative demands of his writing rises to a level of considerable artifice. Other writers invent; Knausgaard remembers."

So fertile is this idea of the relationship between writing and remembering, so natural is the blending of reality and imagination, so appealing is it as a narrative device, that we may begin to speak of a distinct category of recent books devoted to elaborations of it.

Ongoingness: The End of a Diary
by Sarah Manguso
Graywolf Press
Hardcover: $20
Pub: March 2015

For over twenty years, the writer and poet Sarah Manguso kept a detailed diary chronicling the events and experiences of her life. In her latest experimental memoir, *Ongoingness: The End of a Diary,* Manguso assesses her lifelong compulsion to write everything down so that she won't forget it. In breathtaking yet modest vignettes that are each less than a page, Manguso records her impressions while reading her diary entries twenty years later. She begins to understand that her existence is not merely a beginning and an end date, with events in between, but part of a continuum. By exposing the core of what we do when we document our own lives, she discovers that memory is a fickle muse, always in operation, and functioning in two realms, each with limitations. There are *unrecalled* memories: "Left alone in time, memories harden into summaries. The originals become almost irretrievable." And there are *recalled* memories: "The least contaminated memory might exist in the brain of a patient with amnesia—in the brain of someone who cannot contaminate it by remembering it. With each recollection, the memory of it further degrades." The most striking thing about Manguso's personal essay is that it denies the reader full access to her life—the facts of her existence—and, instead, keeps the reader transfixed on her ruminations. We witness her coming to terms with memory's inherent faultiness, revealing the hard work of forming a meaningful identity in a sea of ever-changing memories. We are deprived of the diary and the gritty details therein but the book enlightens without it, because the self-documentation Manguso does share transcends time, place, and the confines of a life.

Self-Portrait in Green
by Marie NDiaye
Translated by Jordan Stump
Two Lines Press
Paperback: $9.95
Pub: November 2014

"How strange it is that this woman you can no longer bear to know so well should suddenly metamorphose on her own into a *green woman*, and one of that type's most alien and troubling of forms." This selection is not from a work of fantasy. It is from award-winning French novelist Marie NDiaye's beautiful, novella-length memoir, *Self-Portrait in Green*, published by Two Lines Press and translated from the French by Jordan Stump. When asked to write her memoir, NDiaye produced, quite literally, a portrait of the color green. Green mysteriously, symbolically embodies women in NDiaye's life: green women haunt her memoir. They appear as women who openly defy mortality by returning from the dead or rising unscathed after a fatal fall. They appear as living, fearless creatures who insert themselves into her life, as unwelcomed social run-ins or as seductresses seducing her father. And most shocking, her own mother transforms into a woman in green right before her eyes. It is clear NDiaye's use of the color green is an attempt to explain an uncontrollable force within a human's identity, but she leaves the reader to interpret the significance of the uncanny color creeping into her life. Nothing is as it seems, timelines are sporadic or nonexistent, and memories are teased out using a fantastical comb. Unlike Manguso, she is not tormented by a faulty memory; she allows it to haunt her and form the imagined landscapes of her reality. The real mingles with the invented, and truth for NDiaye is subjective, fashioned by her own perception. Perhaps this is a way of respecting and exploring the past without being tied to it. The author can be unafraid of making a mistake while exploring her own identity: and readers are left wondering if the writer herself is a green woman.

The Body Where I Was Born
by Guadalupe Nettel
Translated by J.T. Lichtenstein
Seven Stories Press
Hardcover: $22.95
Pub: June 2015

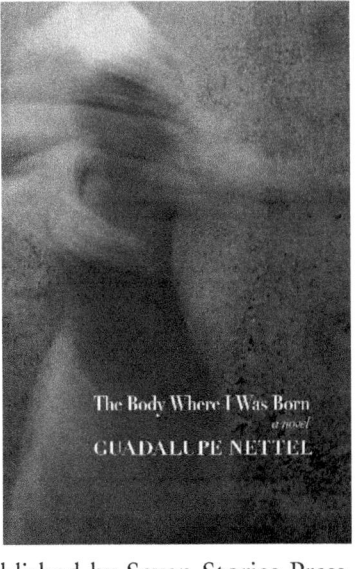

NDiaye demands that the reader suspend disbelief by infusing fantastical elements in her nonfiction work, while Mexican author Guadalupe Nettel, like Knausgaard, dismantles the traditional form of the novel by inserting into her work of fiction a real-life narrative. Her novel *The Body Where I Was Born*, translated by J.T. Lichtenstein and published by Seven Stories Press, begins on a psychoanalyst's couch where a young woman is telling the story of her 1970s childhood—a childhood navigated along the fault lines of a family shaped by politics, the law, and the emotional havoc of a mother intent on fixing her daughter's eye defect. The young narrator in Nettel's story is resilient, strong, and a keen, sensitive observer who becomes skilled at metamorphosing to adapt to changing circumstances—it is fitting that she escapes into books and falls in love with Kafka's *Metamorphosis*. Unlike the crisp, clear narrator in Karl Ove Knausgaard's autobiographical novels, Nettel's narrator experiences a startling new perception of reality, appearing in reflections from the mind of the narrator as a grown woman that are sparing and at times bizarre and obscure—pretending that she is a cockroach becomes a way of dealing with the challenges of having an incurable eye defect. There is not a defiance of physical laws, like

NDiaye's "green women," but the defamiliarization of reality is at work, and Nettel is a master storyteller.

For these authors, and like others who write about their lives, both reality and imagination are simultaneously at work. In the essay "Why Fiction is Good For You," Jonathan Gottschall argues that telling stories has an important effect on society and our evolution, because writing fiction is a tool for processing our emotions and anxieties. The worlds of the real and invented are in flux, because that is what we, as readers and writers, demand of literary landscapes: spaces wherein reality is halted, or slightly transformed, in order to accommodate new rule systems and methodologies. We welcome, perhaps crave, a new headspace, a new perspective of our own present. If stories serve to defamiliarize lived experiences, the writer, in crafting her tales, refracts her perceptions of the world through invented prose, thereby creating something entirely new and unearthly like NDiaye's memoir, or augmenting actual facts, like Nettel and Knausgaard's fiction. Ultimately, then, it might be best to understand *fiction* and *nonfiction* not as genres, but as literary devices—parts of the narratives themselves.

Naming the Parts, and Why I Didn't March with Martin

I always said I would not march unless they would let me carry my shotgun.
— *Archie Byron*

What is blackness but a nose split like two
sides of a feather? One soft for quiet
flight, the other the bone of a knuckle
torn in rage and stinging with its own blood.
My thumbs have pressed eyes and lips of woman
and man together in sawdust and glue,
four legs in one foot. We are all marching,
me with my shotgun and my Grandmamma
quilting my story of three histories
in a single face, her cheekbones like suns
lighting the caves where runaway slaves hid
in her people's graves—black and red wires
spliced together by ignorance. If I
must choose a part of my body to keep,
I'll take one good ear to hear who's coming.

James Cihlar

Why We Hate Mice

You don't know me without you
—Mark Twain, *The Adventures of Huckleberry Finn*

It's not because we know
where there's one there's ten.

It's not because once we see them
they are always there. Of course,

we'd rather not think of their hopeless journeys
through mazes to levers,

or machines that constrict their bodies,
a human ear growing on a mouse's back—

or, for that matter,
a field of cotton growing in the sun,

a forgotten tool in the sand,
a bundle of sticks to start a fire.

In their close-set eyes and low foreheads
we never see our own. It's not because

in their storied lives they outsmart cats,
perpetually turning the contraption

around on the inventor.
Nor do we identify with cartoon cats,

the stooge tormentors.
Although we marvel

at their ingenious ability to collapse
their skeletons as small as a dime,

we will never admire them.
Despite the uses we've put them to,

we hate them still because, bottom line,
they could get along without us.

Autumn Rinaldi

The Fix

The street was full of the people I didn't want to make eye contact with. They were either strung out, begging for anything we had to spare, or just there to be seen, the kind I always called the *scenics* before they were officially called just *scenesters.*

By now most of the crowd had cleared out, the bands stopped playing and the stands were closing, rolling down weather flaps to keep their booths dry for tomorrow. The next day would bring a new band and more junk to sell, and the Imagination Stations would open again, for kids to make art with recycled crepe paper and dried macaroni.

I didn't want to come down here while the festival was going on, and I didn't know if the place would be open this late. But the flashing sign was on—indecipherable down the block, but it was there. Another news story popped up on my home page the other day: companies would soon have to take them down if you couldn't read them legibly within fifty feet. Of course, we didn't know if this was true or how to even regulate this, as everyone's eyesight was different. And then there was the joke: *If you can't read our sign, it's a SIGN you need to come in and get fixed up!*

I didn't need this sort of fix at first; I'd inherited my mother's good vision. She didn't even need reading glasses until she was sixty-six, and even then, she didn't think a procedure was necessary. But her other genetics kicked in. This was back when more and more health care companies were starting to capitalize on replacements, and she was surprised to discover what her plan covered.

"Are you sure you don't want a basic operation?" the consultant asked her. "I don't think you need a whole new colon. Yours can be saved, and we'd much rather give one to someone who *needs* it."

But Mom had argued she *did.* Colon cancer ran on her mother's side of the family, and her physician had just discovered malignant polyps. Her abdomen was a ticking time bomb. "I'd only be prolonging the worst cancer there is . . . and the most painful," she had added. How much truth there was in this, no one knew, but Mom persisted. She waited three weeks to hear back from them, as well as Individual Choice, to see if she was covered.

She was. But that meant she would have a limited amount of organs available to her in the future. After rethinking it, Mom declined the operation. Colon cancer was the only thing she worried about, and she stated she didn't need a single thing as long as she lived. I remember her saying this every time I gave her a gift. *I've got all I need, son. Why'd you have to go buying me anything?*

Mom was true to her word, but she hadn't known she would also inherit a blood disease that made her have to check into the regular hospital for routine blood transfusions until she was dead at sixty-nine. Yet I saw the glimmer of possibility in her eyes that became recognizable in my own, later on.

"I could make it another twenty, if I had the option," she'd said to me before she passed: a pretty painful death, too. "These old doctors are always going on and on about how it's not 'normal' to replace, that Real Science is saving what we have! I say, if what we've got doesn't work, there's no point in keeping it. Patching a tire, plugging a hole, the thing's gonna blow out when you hit a bump. Why not get a brand new car, for the same amount of money, that you *know's* gonna last!"

Mom hadn't lasted. If she'd been able to have a complete blood substitution, she would have. It just didn't exist at the time, and wouldn't, until three years after her death.

I didn't feel the craving until my mid-thirties. I dodged the stuff I'd inherited until one of my blood tests came back that I was pre-diabetic. My doctor recommended a low-carb diet and prescribed a blood-glucose meter, which would be hard to find these days, since there are so many pancreases available. They're still the easiest to grow. Their matter is easy to maintain in a lab, and they don't require as much maintenance as hearts and lungs and eyes, and definitely livers. For some reason, as one of the companies' representatives said in an interview, laughing, livers were finicky. And the highest in demand.

When I got my new pancreas, I lost my meter since there was no reason to check anymore (it'd been a huge pain in the ass to prick my finger twice a day, drop my blood on the strip, use the alcohol wipe, record the numbers: so when that was in the past, I did a dance).

Because I signed the last line of the disclaimer, I got the papers that told the story of my new organ.

It was a grown one, not donated (the donated ones had stories you wouldn't believe!). Enclosed were colored photos of the labs and a hundred-thousand containers of frosted glass, guarded by a proudly beaming young technician holding a clipboard and pen.

But among the Frequently Asked Questions, printed on the back of the brochure, was the standard "How does this happen?" as if there was anyone left on earth who didn't at least know the basics. Ellen and Oprah had the Creator on their talk shows, the man who had the idea, who made the magic happen; he'd explained briefly, in his Armani monkey suit with the brocaded lapels he was famous for wearing around the press, of regenerating matter and creating DNA and cells they'd once thought were "throwawayers." And God, how many articles and interviews had *Time* done on the story? You can't pick up a single *Reader's Digest* without coming across another "Replacement Surgery Saved My Son!" So I didn't bother reading past "Excellent question! We start by simply . . . ."

It wasn't simple, I knew, no matter what *Today's Forensics, People Weekly,* and late-night shows told us, but we knew we didn't *quite* understand it any more than those grinning, green technicians, sans clipboard and pen, photographed outside those frosted glass partitions in advertisements. All I knew is that I had a new pancreas, and a good one, raised behind one of those sterilized frosted glass containers. No more fudging around with finger sticks and ordering a plain oil-and-vinegar salad instead of a baked potato with butter and sour cream.

After that, my body didn't need anything else, and I didn't crave. I'd been born with my mother's genes, which meant I'd probably get colon cancer at sixty-seven, and the blood disease would kick in around sixty-nine. But I'd also inherited my mother's *I wasn't born with it, so I don't need it* attitude.

Until about three years after I'd traded in my malfunctioning pancreas for a new, spiffy one.

I remember the day up in the lodge in the Rockies. The temperatures dropped below zero a few minutes after the sun set, and if you weren't prepared, you could be in big trouble. I didn't realize I was in big trouble until the first signs of frostbite.

"You'd better go in, fast," my friend told me, blinking from the flurries that the wind cast up from the valley. I'd stuck my hand deep in the pocket of my goose-down parka; I'd lost my glove in a nose-dive off of a slope that turned out to be bigger than I'd anticipated. I carried both ski poles in one hand but had to take my hand out of my pocket when one started to slip. By that time, the wind chill was probably negative-fifteen.

When I managed to get myself and my skis into the lodge, I was more worried about my toes--I hadn't felt them since that afternoon— and I pulled my socks off thinking they weren't even there anymore, that they'd just tumble out like ten ice cubes. They were pink, but after a few minutes they started regaining color. Then I looked at my hand. It seemed all right, a little white and pink streaked, but my fingers did not break off like icicles as I'd imagined.

My hand didn't turn dark purple until the next morning.

I had a choice, of course. Either I'd live the rest of my life without a right hand, or I'd get a new one. You *always* heard about the hand surgeries; those were the most popular ones on newsstands, along with eyes and jaws (people were *always* damaging their jaws). And who would *want* to try to get along without it? I would have to teach myself stroke survival techniques and learn how to brush my teeth, hair, and wipe my ass with my left hand.

Or.

Like I said, it was a no-brainer.

Eventually, I understood why there were so many demands for jaws. Folks lost them all the time: in fights, a trip down a flight of concrete stairs, a whop in the mouth, or maybe they didn't like the look of the ones they were born with. I'd gotten two different jaws since the age of forty-three, and I was lucky to get them. The one I'd inherited from my mother was cracked when I was slammed into a subway wall by a fleet of protesters. The second when I went down headfirst on a bus, after the driver slammed on his brakes for a dog.

I told myself I'd never be like Angela Case. She'd been on *The Ellen and Oprah Morning Show* twice and Dr. Phil's show at least a dozen times. She was what they all called "addicted."

I'd once seen a picture of how she'd looked before, with the parts she'd been born with (what they referred to as "originals"). "Originally," she'd been a lanky thing with a long, slim face. In her biography, I read she'd been cursed with every sickness known to man. She had chicken pox twice, the measles, the mumps; plus, she'd worn a back-brace from the time she was nine until she was sixteen. She'd had abnormally heavy periods where she'd pass out in the middle of driving. She said she'd been prone to nosebleeds, too. In other words, Angela had spent a hell of a long time being miserable, and being a human insect with no curves was just the icing on her misery cake.

By her late twenties, she'd done away with the bone structure she hated and stuck out in places where she'd always wanted to stick out. Her new nose belonged to a former supermodel who'd been killed in a car accident and was only damaged from the sternum down. Angela had been in the same city as the accident: in the right place at the right time, she had said in her interviews. By the time she was thirty-two she was on her sixth jaw (none of them ever sat right on her face, she'd said), and who knows how many of everything else. She once said the only parts she owned outright (by that, she meant "originally"), were her brain and heart. She said she didn't want anyone else's heart because she couldn't imagine finding another quite as big as her own, and when it stopped, she would, too. As far as brains went, Angela—when she was thirty-four, at least—was proud of the one she was born with.

I remember the headlines as if they were yesterday's, but my memories are mixed up with the memories of others. That was the thing about surgery we didn't know at first. I've heard it described as phantom pain, a part of you that hasn't disappeared, though the limb has been torn off. Sometimes I feel a bit sick, as if my blood levels are out of whack, even though my new pancreas still does its job, and often I have pain in my new fingertips, as if some imaginary frost is nibbling at them, sometimes gnawing. And I, like Angela Case, have the noodle I was born with: all my memories are my own. But every so often, one filters in from some unknown place, drifting in like the smell of summertime.

But first—the headlines!

"Top expert scientists on the verge of a breakthrough!" That one we'd waited for, probably for a year and a half. Every day was a new headline saying "Breakthrough! Breakthrough!" and we weren't going to believe a thing until we saw it with our own eyes. And when we did . . . .

The first successful replacement brain tissue (note, this was not a donated organ—this was "lab-made!") was performed on a man named Harold Wiser. He was a terminal case. He'd already had three tumors removed, but new ones quickly took their places; they'd said once you get one, that's it, pal. We followed his story like a kid pours over the toy section when the holidays roll around. Harold had only a month at most, and he decided to donate his last thirty days to science.

Harold's successful procedure making the front cover of *Modern Biology* was a no-brainer (no pun intended). And like Angela Case, he was set up to do his share of talk show spots, that is, until it happened. Something they hadn't expected and later chalked up to a minor nervous breakdown. In short, one morning Harold Wiser shot his wife and, soon after, two people on the bus while on the way to his factory job: one of them a little boy his son's age. Just to be safe, they later said, any additional brain tissue procedures on patients were postponed until they discovered the root of Harold's problem. If there was any connection to Harold's killing spree and his newly acquired brain, the media did not disclose it, though debunker websites swear they have "proof."

I wasn't interested in proof at the time—my new hand, new jaw, and new pancreas, that was keeping me from doing the swab-stick-drip-click-record for another fifty years, were doing me great. Science was exploding.

And competing. New companies were sprouting up, and some didn't even require coverage. You paid in monthly installments, and Congress was promising a new kind of "replacement forgiveness plan." I voted in the new President who, during his campaign in Washington, never failed to bring this up, and why not? Some addicts had gone too far and they had no choice sometimes but to move overseas; some even committed suicide. And that caused even more controversy.

The biggest story involved a woman; I forget her name, but she was involved in one of the most horrific accidents of the year. She and her four-year-old daughter were driving down the East Coast on their way to visit her husband, who'd been deployed for over seven years and was stationed on a base in Florida. The roads had iced overnight:

a semi lost control and totaled the woman's SUV. The child was killed instantly, but the mother survived long enough to learn that seven ribs were broken on her left side, the side of the impact, which impaled her organs. Her husband was given permission to leave the base to see her for the last time in an ICU unit somewhere in North Carolina.

But it turned out it wouldn't be for the last time, because a new torso—it had *everything*, I tell you: heart, lungs, the works—became available. They didn't tell the woman, near death, where it'd come from, but even if they had, she would've said what we *all* would've said, *Anything you can do to let me live.*

We are all desperate to keep going.

The lady behind the desk is new; I've only seen her once, so she doesn't know me from Adam's off ox. They might've said something to her about me—people like me. She doesn't give me the look the other ones gave, not yet. You might know the look, or maybe you don't. It's the same one a bartender gives a drunk who strolls in asking for, *Just a little something to help me get home, buddy. I had a day from hell, you understand, right?* The bartender takes pity and gives him a little something. And then another. And all the drunk sees is pity, but the bartender keeps them coming, and eventually pity becomes peripheral.

This lady doesn't give me the look yet, but she will soon. I keep thinking I won't be helped today. It's getting late, and they probably want to close up because of the festival down the block. Probably a busier Saturday than usual. Concert-goers can be the biggest addicts of all. Weed and coke destroy a whole bunch of organs.

I look though a catalog as I wait. I have the same one at home; they send me the new edition every month. Mostly it contains new breakthroughs, but what I like best are advertisements featuring people enjoying life despite their age. They can be seventy, one hundred, and look at them, skiing at the Catskills and partying it up on some yacht in the Caribbean.

But I also like the merchandise.

"Hey, John," I hear. One of the techies, Dr. Lance, a young man fresh out of med school, *summa cum laude*, I know. We'd chatted so many times about how he'd struggled in his third year because he lacked people skills.

He looks beat. A long Saturday, I was sure, staring at a computer and trying to match customers with the best offers, based on insurance and blood type and organ compatibility.

"Like doing taxes, all day, every day," he'd once said.

This location is in danger of closing down because of the new laws giving customers an exchange policy. *One for the other*, the slogan said, and man, did that cause an uproar in Congress.

"It's the people's choice," some argued. "Our bodies!" Others ranted that it promoted a sacrificial agenda. The President himself declared that it took advantage of the desperate people who don't have other means of payment available.

I set my catalog down on the waiting room table, and we go back to the usual room. I've been in them all, at one time or another.

The décor of this one in particular strikes my fancy. They always try to make them homey, and not like a hospital or clinic. After all, this is just a consultation. They bring you to the white rooms when it's time to operate. To replace.

I tell him I need the usual.

Dr. Lance looks even more tired.

"Busy day?" I ask.

"You have no idea," he grumbles. "I'd rather it be busy than not, but we need more staff. And there was a botched Stevie Wonder last week."

A "Stevie Wonder": you can guess what that is.

Lance looks a little regretful confessing confidential information, but I've heard the stories before. He knows I won't blab.

"What happened?" I ask.

"One was fine, the other became dislocated from the socket. By the time she was able to get to the ER, she almost bled to death. Scared her son so bad, he went into shock. I would, too, if I'd never seen it before."

"Damn," I say, and I wait for Dr. Lance to begin.

He leans over the desk and looks me up and down. His freckles make him look younger than he is. I think he might be around my son's age, if I'd been able to have one. "We're running out of places to give you an incision," Lance says. "You know replacement skin can only be cut into a few times. It has a limit. Replacement skin can't regenerate cells at the same rate as your original, so we'll have to stitch over the same seam as before, to eliminate any unnecessary bunching of tissue."

It sounds scarier that it really is, folks.

"I really like the stuff you used before," I say to Lance. Already, the familiar rush is starting; my heart beats a little faster. "I don't suppose you have any more of it?" The man who'd donated the skin I'm using at the time had been an athlete; he'd accidentally overdosed on painkillers.

Lance says, looking pained, "It's too pricey for you right now."

I can't help but chuckle. "Well, hell."

"Are you still having problems with the hand?" Lance knows about my . . . issues.

"None," I lie.

"Are you sure, John? Because we'd rather fix it sooner than later." We both know what "later" means. Remember what I told you about Harold Wiser.

"It's just the little minor things," I say. "I know I'm close to my limit, don't worry." This is a good thing to say.

Dr. Lance looks at me the way a bartender does, when the drunk says, *Just a little bit to help me get home.*

We schedule an appointment three weeks away, and I leave the building; coming from one direction are the remaining folks that stayed till after the band broke down their equipment and loaded it up. I see some burly guys up on scaffolding, removing lights and technical stuff from up high; they look like shadows without faces up there in the darkness against the overcast sky. A group of kids sit on a curb with nowhere to go, it seems, content to hang around until midnight, shooting the breeze and talking about the next day, the next weekend, and the thousand others in their future. I want to tell them there aren't as many as they think.

I can tell already it's going to be one of those nights. I start to struggle as soon as I get into the car. I don't drive on highways anymore because my right hand is so much stronger than the other, which causes twitches only exacerbated by high speeds, and I'm not going to risk killing myself or someone else. A head-on collision is not going to be *my* future.

I think maybe I should've come clean and told Dr. Lance, but I don't want to waste any more on my hand than necessary. I had other plans for what I had left. A whole new hand would wipe me out for the next year. I concentrate on relaxing the muscles in my right wrist and forearm; this often helps control the muscles when they start moving when I don't mean for them to. I think of what the physical therapist told me, of mantras many receivers have been taught.

They belong to you. You have control over them. Not the other way around.

I remember this tonight and it works. Sometimes it doesn't. But I have a good feeling, and good feelings breed even better physical results.

Remember how I told you I have some memories that waft in, like the scent of bathroom cleanser, or a warm, home-cooked meal, that they don't belong to me? I have to concentrate hard to see if they are mine, and with some calculation, I can separate them into two categories: ones that I'd experienced myself and those that belong to my donors. I don't have to worry about my mind—like I'd said, I still have my own. But sometimes one comes in that has nothing to do with anything I can recall experiencing.

The childbirth memory was confirmation of that. The woman's recollection hit me hard one morning when I was in the shower: she had been in the worst pain in her life, pain so bad she'd passed out. When she came to, she saw her baby for the first time and then felt even more pain, because she didn't fall in love with it at first sight like she was supposed to. I remember she felt like the worst person—no, *woman*—in the world, because she had no desire to pick it up and comfort it when it cried for her.

This memory, I think, came from my eyes—yes, I had my own Stevie Wonder done a year and a half ago when my eyesight began to fail, because who wants to look like an old fart with reading glasses?

Another memory came from a man who'd donated his liver (as I'd said, they were in high demand, but I'd been lucky). The papers told me he was a fireman who'd died in a blazing house, but his liver was still good to go. Yet once in a while I'd wake in a sweat, not from a dream, but something close to a dream: I'd seem to feel my skin burning off, the house—not mine—with its hidden voices, voices calling out. It wasn't until I had the dream again that I realized they were calling for me, that they knew I was there to help, that they were running out of time and oxygen.

Sometimes I awake and the fingers of my donated hand are wrapped around my other wrist, as if it might sense its time might be short, or it is jealous of the one I'd been born with and fears its seniority. Maybe it just remembers something I don't.

This night, I would be lucky to be haunted by just memories.

Deep down inside, I feel like I'm just beginning. There are parts of me that are too young to go down with the ship, as they say, and the rest are becoming too worn to keep up.

"John, it's the curse," he says at my checkup. "You can't escape death this way. I don't care what others try to do. It wasn't *designed* for that." But I look at his face and see the doubt of his own words. Because we both know it's true.

It was designed for exactly that.

"Even if you could do it for a little while, would you *want* to?"

And I don't answer; he can read it on my face.

I'm not Angela Case, the human patchwork, as they call her. But I understand why she made a career out of suspended aging; she's now living in Monte Carlo or somewhere, last I'd heard. But I'm not ready to leave. I don't want to meet my father in the afterworld or wherever we end up and find out the truth about him, where he was between the time I was five and when I came across his name online, now a successful engineer. I'm not ready to give up the simple act of breathing, even if it is with someone else's lungs. Somewhere down deep inside of myself is the scent of pine at Christmas, and the ocean when the wind comes across it fast, bringing the scent of salt and fishing boats. A time when time ran slower and I actually felt seconds go by, but now they've become years mixed up with senses belonging to whatever new piece I got last month. Back then, we saw life up close: the seam of a blade of grass, the creases in white sheets after being unfolded, and fuzzy fibers on a blanket on a cold winter morning; the pattern of your wallpaper and faces we made out of them when our eyes were blurry with sleep.

We don't make faces out of things anymore. We've wiped out seconds and moments and replaced them with hours, days, and years, and fake parts.

But I need more of them, to keep feeling alive.

It is three days before the big one. After this, they said (with that silly warning in their voices you'd tell a drunk: *Okay, but just ONE more drink, and that's all*) this is it, now, no more. No excuses, and it didn't matter what my insurance company said. It didn't matter that I even said I'd give up a kidney (aside from livers, these were hot commodities).

The rush of change, of another rebirth, is already pumping through me like crazy, and along with it, a surge of bittersweetness. Like one of those phantom pains, I can recall an old commercial jingle at my grandparents' house on Thanksgiving, sneaking olives from the table before anyone was allowed to eat, and sharing them discretely with my Uncle Nick. And crackly news broadcasts, antennas I had to adjust. TV static, stations calling it quits for the night to doze along with you, but not before the national anthem. And real Christmas trees. The world is so shiny now, so bright and crisp and *seamless*.

It's odd that I can't stop thinking about seams.

I savor the upcoming surge of adrenaline and try not to think that after it's all over, it might be a long time before I might get another one. Until then, I'll have to try to find another way to get it. But my body isn't mine anymore, and even though all this stuff is *new*, it *feels* less. I don't even notice when I accidentally touch a hot pan on the stove, or drip boiling tea on my leg. My world's stripped of senses, and my new body feels numb. Some people say that's the best part. I don't know. All the bodies and faces around me change from one day to the next. There's no way to tell who's young or old anymore. Just the other day, I couldn't tell if I was flirting with a woman who was sixteen or sixty. I can't remember the last time I heard someone talk about a smelly bus stop, or watched a child pet a cat for the simple act of stroking it to discover how soft or shabby its fur is. I don't even recognize my own friends when I pass them on the street. One day I might not even recognize myself.

But I know this will fix it. As they say, the brain gets used to habitual sensation until you have to find a new way to stimulate it. Gone will be the useless memories of when the world was real and not a projection of lights and screens, and where people had their original flesh, not grown parts from a lab. Before, when all of us talked about things other than the parts of us we have to replace soon. New technologies are always on the horizon to make it all brighter and crisper, with less creases and blemishes. Someday they're going to get it perfect.

I hope the new one I get is perfect and prepared to join me in this next stage of my life. I'm sure it will be perfectly content with this new world. And by the time *that* new piece of me gets nostalgic, I know they'll let me come back and get fixed again.

From Our Window
Somewhere in Washington

We sleep near a river
Of ghosts. We watch
Souls exit through
The cracked chimneys
Of neighbor's homes
Like teakettle steam
To let the water's
Current take them
Into shadows cast
By the canopy trees.
We hear them sing
Haunting chants,
Howl to the moon
Or god, or both
As they float past
Our house. Clawing
At the peat and twigs
Clumped to the banks,
We make up
Crude stories about how
They wound up in the river;
We were young and
Forgot everything
Has a life.

Cindy King

The Spires

When the sun came up in Youngstown that night you had already
     taken
your lover's Mustang and were driving south on State Route 62,
gentrified by a short-lived antidote of bourbon and bravado,
and looking forward, you saw a murky, stingy, dishwater dark, and
the wisps of snow on the ground and in headlights made the
     darkness
inferential and ordinary as it sunk into yellowing pastures and the
     goldenrod,
thistle, and dandelion confettied by a county brush hog stalled at the
     roadside,
and the wide road stretched lazily as if it, too, were cut by a brush
     hog; and nothing
kept the sunlight from coming in, the trees leafless and small, the
     cattle ponds growing bright
at just the thought of sun, and the gray earth sustaining a few broken
     down barns
and outbuildings that leaned shoulder to shoulder to support each
     other
in business or blood, though up from them a conclave of farm
     houses, myopic and white,
squinted at cars, and dirt paths and driveways wondered in and out
of the maples and ash; and on that road that was now only partly
     obscured by darkness
due to the brisk migraine light of morning, you could see a few
     steeples touched
with snow so that their spires were shagged and patchy with white;
and they seemed, in silhouette, against the wide overcast sky of Stark
     County, Ohio,
like lofty ambitions, huge and luminous, grounded by the prudence
     of their stocky
brick buildings and raised against idleness, loneliness, and endless
     winters

with unintended allure, like the curses of a woman whose house has
        no power,
who drives a horse-drawn buggy beneath a bonnet, which is dark
        enough,
she thinks, to hide her thoughts from God.

ONE-TWEET FICTION

During our inaugural reading period, we offered five free print subscriptions to our favorite 140-character stories. We were amazed at the creativity you brought to this challenging task. Though we would have loved to award every entry (well, *most* entries), we had to choose five. Here are our favorites:

FORREST DYLAN BRYANT

"Go."
"What's over there?"
"Obscurity. Failure. Rejection. With luck, a few cents per word."
I went, smiling.

AUDREY T. CARROLL

The lake swallowed his scream. Manicured nails (talons) pierced his neck. Instinct drove; she wouldn't lose her son to him.

JENNIFER RUTH JACKSON

She feeds Mother grapes, aiming them past moving, chapped lips. Criticisms, even now. Juice drops turn to wine on her skin.

DAVID JAMES POISSANT

Before the thrown glass, the words they can't take back, before the fist, that kiss, the other loves, there was only, I do.

CHAD SIMPSON

At the talent show, she played a mime. Sat on a bucket, baited an invisible hook. Then cast deep, braced for a fight.

Welcome to Sisyphus, Missouri

We sat in our homes over bologna salad, fried crappy, and breast filet sandwiches from Jay's Crispy Fried Chicken. We looked to one another for assurance that this was not legal. Someone, somewhere had overstepped the bounds. We all agreed it sounded as such and our muscles relaxed, our breathing slowed. Then, the old man in the corner, who always sat with his cowboy hat atop his knee, reminded us about that sheriff down in Arizona. Tent cities. Hundred-degree temperatures. The program's popularity so far-reaching and so great, its fans ordered T-shirts and coffee mugs with the jail's logo printed on them. This information did not help.

That night, as we drank chocolate malts from Cream Castle, water from the faucet, soda held by shaky hands, we talked our throats hoarse. Those of us with DUIs and DWIs spoke of our rights as Sikestonians, our rights as Missourians, our rights as Americans. We had already called our lawyers, those whose likenesses appeared on billboards along the interstate, their chemically treated smiles shining down from high overhead. Those of us who could afford no such call would be appointed an attorney when the time came, the same as the last time, as each time before.

Folks against drinking all together spoke of God's hand in this, of joining re-election campaigns, of how refreshing it was to see our elected officials working for us. We called the 1-800 number for Speak Out down at the *Standard Democrat*, filed our beliefs with the young lady who answered the phone there. The paper ran three of these the day following the law's passage:

Left Busted By a Drunk Driver
I just wanted to say what a mighty fine job those boys in the city hall are doing. My car got run into off Highway Hh two months back by a drunk driver and the man that hit me tried to tell me I had crashed into him. Of course, he was living off the government and had a nicer car than mine. But

guess what? He didn't have insurance. I got stuck with the bill. And he got community service. Saw him picking up trash off the side of the same road where he hit me, not a mile and a half down from my house.

What's This World Coming To?
First, they have us rolling a rock up a hill, then what? We can't drink a beer in our homes? We can't smoke a cigarette on the sidewalk? We can't raise our kids up how we want to? If Canada wasn't a socialist paradise, I'd move north.

It's Time For a Change
I think what they've done here is good for the community. While it isn't funneling money into rehabilitation programs, which we desperately need more of in this state, at least something will be done about this growing societal problem. No law will completely stop the epidemic of alcoholism, but maybe it's time for those who drive intoxicated to be brought to the light, to be publicly ridiculed here in front of the whole of Sikeston.

The demand for the paper was greater than when they printed the Black Friday sale bills each year, greater than '95 when the O.J. Simpson verdict was rendered.

Those of us who had already been caught drinking and driving once or twice—three, four, or five times—dug our feet into our sodded yards, into the dirt, crabgrass, and gravel, and wondered aloud who would be the first. We vowed it would not be us and were quick to turn attention to the next person down the line. To break the monotony of not drinking, to squelch our rising thirst, we formed betting pools and threw down portions of our hard-earned paychecks on dates and people we knew.

Most found solace this way—spending time in the company of friends—but some of us were more nervous and strayed far and wide from the conversations of others. We knew whose name was broached in their circles. When we went to Piggly Wiggly, it did not help to hear our names spoken from two aisles over. We knew these voices because we had grown up with them—had known them the entirety of our lives—but they never knew we heard them. We went home without ever speaking a word.

In not-so-silent anticipation, we waited for the newspaper's morning slap against the stoop, for the *Heartland News* to come on in the evening, for it to start again at ten, while we lay between flat and fitted sheets. With our pillows tucked beneath our heads, we felt safe. We slept those nights with the assurance that this was still a "we" problem.

A week after the law went into effect, a good friend of mine, Pete Pratchard, lost his son in an automobile accident. The boy, Little Peter, had been driving fast, but not too fast, when he blew a tire. His car went into the median between lanes and crashed into the center divider.

I went over to Big Peter's house, rode with him to identify his boy. It was not pretty. A sight I will never, ever get out of my head. With that image smothering every inclination, every decision, every action, we went down to The Well.

There wasn't anybody down there but the bartender and the man in the cowboy hat. I nodded politely and ordered a couple of beers. Pete racked a game of nine-ball and over the night those couple beers turned into twenty-dollar games at the table and a half bottle of whiskey apiece.

When Big Peter struck the nine ball and the cue hopped from the table and skidded across the floor, I didn't take his cash from the table and put it in my pocket.

"Hit it again," I told him. It was an honest gesture toward a grieving father.

"Don't pity me," Pete said. "You've been doing it all night."

I thought about his words, and it didn't take long for me to figure how right they were. I did pity him. I pitied the way he told funny stories about his son's awkwardness around girls. I pitied the way he laughed to avoid crying. I pitied the hole left where his life should have been.

"You're not in the right frame of mind to be deciding how to take anything one way or the other," I said.

He didn't hit me. He didn't spit in my face. He stepped close to me, up until we were just about nose to nose, and he said, "Don't come to my son's funeral. I don't want you there."

That was it. He stepped away from me and walked to the bar. When Dan refused his money, Big Peter walked out mumbling about bullshit friends and stepping on peckers. I looked from the door to Dan, to the grizzled old man with the cowboy hat. I went and sat next to him. Big Peter was gone and I wasn't running after him. I wasn't about to chase after anyone. My second wife could attest to that more than any person living or dead.

Young ones always do draw a crowd and Little Peter was no different. More than a hundred gathered within the confines of Unity Village. The paved lane weaving through the cemetery nearly burst with the number of cars lined end-to-end along its length. Instead of driving my GMC pickup over there and finding a spot among the rest, I parked across the street in the Mexican restaurant's parking lot and watched through binoculars. While I knew I was not wanted, and that I would not be seen by those in attendance, I dressed in the only suit I owned, wore the only pair of cufflinks I had ever purchased—real working levels with green fluorescent liquid inside.

As those with chairs were seated, I retrieved the pint of Jack Daniel's from the glove box and drank. I put my feet up on the bench seat and took swig after swig until the last words had been cast and the crowd fanned out to their cars. Through the binoculars—through the herd of people walking away from the gravesite—I caught a glimpse of Big Peter hugging his ex-wife. I put the bottle to my lips and tilted it back. I drank until it held no more of its amber glow.

Tapping at my driver's side window woke me. Disoriented, I hoped it was Big Peter creating the racket. I was sorely disappointed when I looked up and spied the uniform. It was so dark I might have mistaken it for black had past experience not taught me it was navy. I cranked the window down.

"What can I do for you, Officer?" His name tag read Jones. He was a younger man. Around Little Peter's age. I did not recognize him.

"Turn off the ignition. Slowly, now. No sudden movements or anything like that." I did as I was told. "Now, open the door and step from the vehicle." I put my hand on the door handle before I looked back to him.

"What's this about?" I said.

"Just come on from the vehicle and we'll discuss it out here." I stepped from the truck's cab—my right foot catching on the loose trim along the door—and I almost fell. Officer Jones shut the door behind me.

"I'm not going to ask if you've been drinking. The smell and that little display are enough to answer that one. But I am going to ask if you're willing to take a breathalyzer."

I didn't answer because he hadn't asked me a question. He tapped me three times on the shoulder with his index finger. "Hello," he said. "Hello? Hello." Before I could turn from him, I vomited all over his shiny black shoes.

I was handcuffed, driven to the station, booked, and left to sit in a cell with those whose lives had been tougher than I could imagine. I thought I was lucky to have been allowed to keep my shoe laces and cufflinks—that Mark Riggins at booking had done me a great favor by allowing me to hold onto my possessions—but it wasn't long before a man whose skin clung to his bones like vacuum packed steak asked to see my cufflinks. I kept my head down and raised an arm. But he didn't mean see as in see with your eyes; he meant see as in take them from my shirt and give them to him. I obliged, handing him a cufflink. Knowing I would never hold possession over it again, I passed him the second as well.

Over the next two hours the man made sure the walls and floor, each of the bars both horizontal and vertical, the toilet and washbasin, that all of these were level. As he did so, he muttered to himself about lines and ancient geometry, the New Madrid fault and the Big One. His constant movement made me dizzy; his constant chirping, headache inducing. I had no relief from him until the guard came to the door and called my name. Because I believed I had no one, no one to care about me, no one to post my bail, I was surprised to see Big Peter. He rose from a chair in the waiting room as the officer opened the thick metal door between geometry and freedom.

When we were outside and situated in his truck, Big Peter turned to me. "Today is the day I was supposed to bury my son. I did that," he said. "After, I was supposed to go back to the house and drink until

I never had a son or an ex-wife. But instead, here I am, bailing your sorry ass out of jail. Tell me why on earth that is, why I'm here. Really. I don't have the answer."

I kept my head down as I had when the man asked to see my cufflink. Big Peter put the car in reverse and pulled from the police station's parking lot. Everything he said was true. He needed to grieve for his boy, and I had gotten in the way of that. "I'm sorry," I said. It was all I could manage in the moment and it was not nearly enough, I knew.

"I battled with myself over whether or not to come. But it was bullshit. I saw it all play out. It wasn't right."

I stared through the window at the hedge apple and sweet gum trees lining North Kingshighway, at their fruits littering the ground. I thought about my grandmother placing the large green balls around the windows of her house to keep the bugs out. I thought about the gumball fights we had as children. I wanted to go back to that, to the time when punishment for doing the same thing over and over again might have been a whooping, but never amounted to anything more.

"You weren't even driving," he said.

On the one hand, Big Peter was right; I hadn't been driving. But I knew better. I knew to turn the car off and take the keys from the ignition. I knew that not doing this would be viewed the same as operating the vehicle under the influence. But I did not argue with him. I continued to stare out the window, thinking of my grandmother's house where I was raised, thinking of how she would view me sitting here in this truck, smelling of vomit and jail.

When Big Peter dropped me at the end of my drive, he lingered. I looked back as I opened the front door and wondered if he wanted to come in, if he wanted me to get back in the truck and ride home with him. I wondered if the same thought ran through his mind that would soon sweep through the community of drinkers across Sikeston: at least it wasn't me.

At the trial, it wasn't a matter of whether I was guilty so much as whether or not I would be sentenced in accordance with the Sisyphus Law. My lawyer, Mr. Innocent from the brightly colored roadside billboards, had worked as the judge's clerk for a decade before going to law school. It seemed, in the week leading up to my court appearance, I would receive a Suspended Imposition of Sentence and with it face a $1,000 fine, SATOP classes, community service, and probation. But, after I had pled guilty as part of the deal made between Mr. Innocent and the judge, the Honorable Charles W. Maxwell took off his glasses and cleared his throat.

"This will be your second DWI conviction within the last five years," he said. I remained silent. I knew better than to speak without being asked in a court of law.

"With that said, your lawyer, Mr. Wilhelm, and I have discussed your case at length and have come to an arrangement." He paused. "In lieu of jail time, or probation, I recommend, in accordance with Section 342.056 of the Municipal Code of Sikeston, Missouri, you be sentenced to rolling a boulder, not exceeding two hundred and fifty pounds, up and back down the Sikeston Ridge on Salcedo Road until the duration of eight hours has been completed." He banged his gavel and stood.

I looked to my lawyer, pleaded with my eyes for him to do something, anything. I felt he had sold me out, that my city, state, and country had betrayed me. He shrugged.

"Go through with the punishment. Let them have their way," he said. He winked at me and I was ready to haul off and punch him. If I didn't stop to realize where I was, I might have done just that. But judges don't take kindly to those who punch lawyers in their courtrooms. I walked without looking back. I had no choice. I would be the first.

Four days after my court appearance, I was informed through an automated telephone call that the date and time had been set for the execution of my sentence. Hours later, my phone rang. It did not stop. CNN, MSNBC, FOX News, Al Jazeera, CBS, ABC, *The Washington Post*, *The Seattle Times*, the *St. Louis Post-Dispatch*, KFVS 12, the *Standard Democrat*, and so many others from near and far couldn't help but trip over one another to get an exclusive with the man who would become Sisyphus in little over a week. I tried to phone my lawyer, but when I picked up the receiver, I accidentally answered a call. It was a woman speaking through a thick accent asking if she could have a quote for France 24.

I hung up and dialed Mr. Innocent's number. I wanted to know if there was anything we could do to push back the date, to stop the harassment, to put an end to all of this.

"You don't want to do that," he said. "I have a plan."

"Great," I said. "You have a plan. That makes me feel worlds better."

"Wear something nice," he told me. "Drink plenty of water the day before. Trust me." I hung up without responding.

That night, I unplugged the telephone but could still hear it ringing. Outside, news vans raised antennas, reporters trampled my lawn. In the kitchen, I looked to the liquor cabinet and realized it was empty. In the bathroom was mouthwash. I unscrewed the lid and tipped the bottle back.

When the morning of my public shaming came, my lawyer was escorted down the street by two marked police cars. I watched through the front window as the sea of reporters and slack jaws parted before them. I wore my suit. I had no cufflinks.

The knock at the door didn't so much surprise me as it did meld the reality of the situation into my brain. At the threshold of my home, my lawyer stood shoulder to shoulder with four police officers.

"Are you ready for this?" Mr. Innocent said. I didn't answer but stepped past him. The officers formed a tight phalanx around us but could not stop the microphones from being hurled at my face. They could not stop the angry chants somewhere deep in the background that likened me to child molesters and terrorists. They could not stop the fear building deep down inside of me.

The drive to the Sikeston Ridge was only five minutes and the wind from the open window felt good against my pale face. I had an entourage seventy-five cars deep. A black SUV sped past us on the shoulder and a man with an embarrassment of a beard hung from the back driver's side window with his camera. The police car behind ours took off after them. I lost track of both vehicles as they turned down a side street. The sky stretched out pink and orange beyond the ridge.

When I stepped from the cruiser and saw the stone, I was disappointed. For some reason, when I imagined two hundred and fifty pounds, I thought of something grandiose. But the rock hardly reached my knees.

At the bottom of the hill, I stood next to it as reporters and townsfolk filed down the Ridge, as photographers snapped pictures. Before the Mayor said his words about justice being done, about a city's obligation to its citizens, a leather band was led from the rock and fastened to my ankle. When he finished speaking, it was my turn. All eyes were on me.

In place of words, I bent at the knees, the waist, and pushed the rock up the hill for the first time. The crowd followed and then passed me. When I had scaled the hundred and fifty feet to the top, more pictures clicked off. The Mayor put his black wingtip to the rock and kicked it back down the hill. I followed behind it, rolling, twisting, hitting elbows, knees, and the back my head on concrete as I went. The hill was not steep enough for me to roll all the way to its bottom. I stopped halfway, hurting everywhere, but I got to my feet immediately.

When I looked to the top of the hill, the Mayor smiled down at me. He tilted his head and waved the way politicians and beauty queens are taught. I wiped my eyes with the back of my hand and pushed the stone. Again, he kicked it down the hill. In total, I tumbled after the stone three times on account of his shoe and no one stopping him.

Before stepping from the middle of the road, before leaving for more pressing business, the Mayor posed for pictures just out of arm's length. When he was gone, I took the suit coat from my back, folded it, and laid it as nicely as I could at the bottom of the Ridge. My nose bled. My index finger had been dislocated in the second fall. I was pretty sure I knew where the Mayor lived in case I needed to settle that score later.

By lunch, the crowd had thinned by half. I was allowed to sit for thirty minutes and was served two burgers from Kirby's Sandwich Shop, the same as I would have eaten had I been sentenced to jail time. Red Kirby had delivered his burgers every day to inmates until he passed away. In his memory, Red's daughter had taken up this act of kindness. I thanked her for her generosity and unwrapped the first burger. Even though I didn't live but four minutes from downtown Sikeston, I had not eaten one in five or six years. The burgers almost brought tears to my eyes, and not because they were so heavily loaded with onions.

When the break was through, and I had shed my shirt against the late-season sun, I picked up where I left off. I rolled the stone until blisters rose and burst, until blood dripped down my wrists and dried. I rolled the stone until the only spectators left were those with picket signs against drunk driving and the ones who were forced to be there on account of their jobs. At four o'clock, I was down on one knee, almost to the top of the hill again. Time was called by Judge Maxwell, but I stood and pushed. When I was finished, the stone sat on part of the road flat enough to keep it from rolling down once more.

EMTs had been on duty throughout the day and now stepped forward to cleanse and treat my wounds. They checked my heart rate and blood pressure. They splinted my finger. When they declared my vitals fine, I was released to go home. A few reporters waited outside my house, but only a fraction of what had been there at the beginning. I had already become old news. They were off to the next story.

Over the coming months, Mr. Innocent's plan revealed itself. He would charge in suit that the city of Sikeston, Missouri, had inflicted upon me a punishment both cruel and unusual. A slew of legal experts from as far away as Cambridge, Massachusetts, stepped forward to volunteer their services. When they were immediately dismissed, it became apparent what role Mr. Innocent saw for himself in the ending of my story.

As he focused on filing brief after brief, I tried to get upright. Reaching sobriety would have been difficult enough if I had been able to distract myself from the mood swings, the headaches, the tension so tight in my limbs I grew sure my muscles would snap. I could not leave my house. When I did, conversations stopped. People I had known forever turned away from me. There was always someone there to tell me to take my punishment like a man. I could not even read the paper without seeing statements to the effect that I deserved to rot in hell for what I was trying to do to their home, for what I was attempting to do to Sikeston.

Mr. Innocent understood none of this. When he checked in, it was always to let me know of the good news surrounding the case. While he stated in motion after motion that my psychological health had wavered severely since our first encounter, he never once asked me how I was handling the weight of all of this. I never received so much as a, *How are you holding up, Slugger?*

His words, both spoken and written, formed the image of black wingtip on gray stone so many times I dreamed of it. Many nights, my whole being was wrapped inside the stone kicked down the hill. Other times, I was the shoe. And still others, the day played out exactly as it had happened. I woke from these dreams drenched in sweat, unable to sleep again until I had swigged from the bottle once more, twice more, until the bottle had been drained and discarded beneath the couch or in the trash can.

When I told Mr. Innocent about my struggles, he spoke of the mayor and judge as if they were personally responsible for my relapses. When I mentioned I had no means to reimburse him for his services, he scoffed at my assumption that his efforts had been about money. "I'm here to make sure justice has been served on your behalf," he said. "We're in this together," he added.

On the second anniversary of Little Peter's death, I was informed that the Supreme Court of Missouri would hear my case. I found this out not from Mr. Innocent, but from reporters' phone calls insisting I comment on the latest news.

The court date was not for another month but that afternoon picketers took their places on my lawn and on the lawns of my neighbors. Camera crews hoisted antennas. I looked through the blinds and wondered, aloud, how I might live like this for another thirty days.

The phone rang. The crowd's chants played on a loop outside my window. I made it almost a week. By midnight on the sixth day of the circus, I had emptied another bottle of Evan Williams and taken my shotgun from the hall closet. When I had loaded the shells and written my note—a half page apology to whoever might clean my remains from the carpet and walls—I sat in the floor of the living room.

When the doorbell rang, I braced the stock of the gun against my foot. I cried. Every time I cry. The doorbell is replaced by fists pounding on the door. I push the trigger with my toe. I never hear the shot. I never find out who's making all that noise at the door. There's a brief pause of darkness. The movie starts anew, the opening credits rolling not over the news of the Sisyphus Law's passage but over the pool table.

Big Peter skips the ball off the table. I tell him to hit it again. And it all plays out as it always has, as it always will, I suppose. I know the mistakes I've made. I've made them a thousand times now. I don't hide the truth from myself. Not anymore. I see them. All of them. I should stop my drinking. I should shut off the engine. I should never hire Mr. Innoncent. Never let him have his way with pushing the lawsuit against the town. Over and over again I return to these mistakes and for a number of times, a great number of times through them, I wished I could pull the trigger right there after going home from the bar the night Little Peter dies. But you can't do that. And eventually you realize this as carved fact. When you get here, to this realization, not just in thought, but in a way your body can process in its marrow, moments of light present themselves. Maybe you didn't see the cop's reaction the first time you threw up on his boots. Maybe you didn't appreciate the memories of your childhood, of your grandmother, enough. Maybe the world really is just geometry. Hey, you never have to worry about the Big One. The earthquake that will destroy whole towns. There's something to be thankful for. Right there. And today, for this time through, it's enough.

Documentality

1. Hope 4 All Treatment Center

Date: 4.11.16, 50 minute session

Client Identification Number: M4005-64534

Name: Rae Anne Crane

Diagnosis: Axis I: 309.81 Posttraumatic Stress Disorder, 300.7 Body Dysmorphic Disorder; Axis II: 301.83 Borderline Personality Disorder.

Subjective: "I'm still having nightmares and flashbacks. But I'm eating okay and I haven't cut myself."

Objective: R. arrived on time. Clothing two sizes too large for the client, but personal hygiene had improved. States she took all her medication as prescribed. Smiled as she delivered her weekly food and feelings diary. Showed me her completed entries for 12 meals. Reports respecting the terms of the restraining order. Says she has reduced time looking into the mirror to less than an hour a day. Read one chapter of PTSD maintenance text. Reported a feeling of being "unreal" after two pages and stopped reading.

Assessment: Engaged in discussing her spousal abuse history. Reported experiencing insight into the nature of her previous relationship. Said she had confused love and pity, and would be more cautious at who she allows into her life.

Plan: Treatment plan goal 1, refrain from self-harm, continues to be met. Treatment plan goal 2, document progress, continues to be met. Practitioner: Sondra Gray, LICSW

2. Fairfield Apartment Complex, Security Log, Shift Report

Date and time: 4-14-2016, 9:30 P.M.

Incident Location: Apartment 110

Resident: Rayanne S. Crane

Responders: I called Officer B. Adelman, Danfield County Sheriff, but the perp had left by the time the officer arrived.

Mr. Raphael Jackson of apt. 108 called the office to report a noise complaint. When I got there, the door was partially open. Mrs. Crane wore just underpants. She held two barbeque tools, a big fork and a spatula. A half-dressed man she called her "dead husband" held a table leg. Mr. Crane said he was trying to defend himself from her. He put the table leg down and showed me the scratches on his chest.

Mrs. Crane said that there was a restraining order on Mr. Crane. She admitted she let him in because he said he had won money and wanted to share his winnings. Mr. Crane waved the table leg at me. He said Mrs. Crane had called him and invited him to her home for sex. He said that she scratched him after stealing money from his wallet.

I told Mr. Crane he had to leave the premises immediately. He said Mrs. Crane had taken his cash and stuffed it in her underpants. He insisted I look for it, but I refused. I told him he had to leave. I threatened to call the sheriff. Within minutes, Mr. Crane was gone. His license plate number is GA 612EPY. The rest of the night was quiet.

Signature: Rick Victorino

3. Bazooms! Sports Bar, Personnel Action Form

Formal Reprimand: Raeanne Crane drew porn images over urinals when she was cleaning the men's room. She agreed to buy Mark-Off for the walls and remove the graffiti on her own time. She apologized and I know she meant it. I would have fired her but the customers enjoy her personality.

Signature: Rocky McConnell, Shift Manager

Date: 4/16/16

4. Hope 4 All Treatment Center

Date: 4.18.16, 50 minute session

Client Identification Number: M4005-64534

Name: Rae Anne Crane

Diagnosis: Axis I: 309.81 Posttraumatic Stress Disorder, 300.7 Body Dysmorphic Disorder; Axis II: 301.83 Borderline Personality Disorder.

Client called in twenty-four hours prior to her appointment to cancel. Called during her usual appointment time. Client reports an uneventful week. Intends to attend her biological father's concert on 4.21. I reminded her of her past history with Bill Crane. Client stated she felt attendance could be instrumental to her healing.

Practitioner: Sondra Gray, LICSW

5. Excerpt from the autobiography of Bill Crane, *Revolutionary Rock*, published 2017, Ithaca Press

In April of 2016, I met my long-lost daughter Rae Ann. Considering my relationship with her mother, I suppose I should have expected an unhinged moment. Rae Ann did not disappoint. She accused me of heinous crimes against her. She's messed up. I guess I should have been there for her. Being on tour eleven months out of the year took its toll on my family. I probably shouldn't have had a child. Hindsight is always 20/20. Enough about that....

6. Interview with Rayleen Crane, published in *Rolling Stone*, July 2018

MRS. CRANE: I was blind not to see what Bill did to her. He can put whatever spin he wants on his actions, but Rae Anne wouldn't have been as sick if he hadn't hurt her. I blame him. He can take his damn autobiography full of lies and shove it.

7. Hope 4 All Treatment Center

Date: 8.11.18

Client Identification Number: M4005-64534

Name: Rae Anne Crane

Case closed.

Practitioner: Sondra Gray, LICSW

Crossing it Off

Lists are for remembering
things that you would other-
wise forget (so how important
could they be?): stamps, mineral
water, fix the headlight on the car.
The longer the list, the harder
it is to complete, the easier
it is to miss something—usually
vital, like potatoes for
Thanksgiving or having children.
I used to write on the back of
my hand to remember: garbage,
dog food, take medication. But
the ink smudged and blurred
through the day—was that soap
or soup I needed so much?
Then I put notes around
the house—on the coffee pot,
computer screen, taped to
shoe laces: pick up paint
(butternut squash, two gallons),
call the plumber (again, again),
fall in love, etcetera.

CONTRIBUTOR NOTES

CHUCK AUGELLO lives in New Jersey with his wife, three cats, and several unnamed birds that inhabit the backyard. His work has appeared in *One Story, Hobart, Juked, Smokelong Quarterly,* and other fine journals. He is Fiction Editor at *Cease, Cows* and editor of The Daily Vonnegut, (www.thedailyvonnegut.com), a website exploring the work of Kurt Vonnegut.

STACEY BALKUN, author of *Lost City Museum* (ELJ Publications, 2016), earned her MFA at Fresno State. A 2015 Hambidge Fellow, Stacey served as Artist-in-Residence at the Great Smoky Mountains National Park. Her work has appeared in *Gargoyle, Muzzle, THRUSH, Tahoma Literary Review,* and *Bayou,* among others. She writes for *The California Journal of Women Writers* at www.tcjww.org.

HALIE BINSTOCK is a student, living and working in the Boston area. *The Indianola Review* is her first print publication.

CATHERINE A. BRERETON is English, but moved to America in 2008, where she is now an MFA candidate at the University of Kentucky. She writes nonfiction and fiction, primarily, poetry on the odd occasion. Her essay, "Trance," published by *SLICE* magazine in 2014, is listed as a Notable Essay in the *Best American Essays,* 2015. More of her work can be found online in *Literary Orphans* and *Every Father's Daughter,* or in print in *Graze, Glitterwolf,* and other publications. Catherine is the current Editor-in-Chief of *Limestone,* the University of Kentucky's literary journal. She lives in Lexington with her wife and their teenage daughters.

TARA CAMPBELL is a Washington, D.C.-based writer of crossover sci-fi. With a BA in English and an MA in German Language and Literature, she has a demonstrated aversion to money and power. Originally from Anchorage, Alaska, Tara has also lived in Oregon, Ohio, New York, Germany, and Austria. Her fiction has appeared in publications such as *Lorelei Signal, Punchnel's, GlassFire*

Magazine, the WiFiles, Silverthought Online, Toasted Cake Podcast, Litro Magazine, Luna Station Quarterly, the Master's Review and Sci-Fi Romance Quarterly. www.taracampbell.com

EMBE CHARPENTIER is an ESL teacher by day and a writer by night. She's been published fifteen times this year in online and print magazines, including *LitroNY, Polychrome Ink, and Gambling the Aisle.* Her novella, *Beloved Dead,* will be published by Kellan Books. She finds joy in mentoring young writers.

JAMES CIHLAR is the author of the poetry books *Rancho Nostalgia* and *Undoing,* and the chapbooks *A Conversation with My Imaginary Daughter* and *Metaphysical Bailout.* His writing has appeared in *The American Poetry Review, Lambda Literary Review, Prairie Schooner,* and *The Threepenny Review.* He teaches literature courses at the University of Minnesota, and his website is www.jimcihlar.com.

COURTNEY DRUZ lives in Israel and is the author of several books of poetry, including *The Ritual Word* and *The Light and the Light.* She holds a BA in Religious Studies from Brown University and a Master of Architecture degree from the University of Pennsylvania. Her poems have appeared or are forthcoming in *The Adirondack Review, Euphony, The Ilanot Review, The Inflectionist Review, Specs,* and elsewhere.

TIMOTHY DUFFY is a poet and scholar in Connecticut. His poems have appeared in *The Cortland Review, Bop Dead City, Open Letters Monthly, The Lehigh Valley Vanguard, The Eunoia Review,* and elsewhere.

KYLE ENSRUDE is a screenwriter, poet, and fiction writer from Minnesota. He's had one short story published, in Procyon Press's 2014 Short Story Anthology, and has had multiple poetry publications, including *Upper Mississippi Harvest* and *Kaleidoscope.* He also has a set of poems featured in the online gallery, *Spirit Wind Poetry.*

KATE FADICK's chapbook, *SLIPSTREAM* (Finishing Line Press), was released in March 2013. She's been published in several regional print and online journals, including *Pine Mountain Sand and Gravel, Kuduz, Wind'97*, and *American Buddhist Review.*

NADA FARIS is a Kuwaiti writer and performance poet who's finished in the top two positions in six national poetry competitions. In 2012, her article "Every Child Deserves a Home: Zeina Al-Sultan Unveils the Truths Behind Adoption in Kuwait" won the Voice of Success program by *en.v Earth* magazine. In 2013, she represented Kuwait in London's Shubbak Festival, an event that is supported by the mayor of London, and at Iowa's International Writing Program, a ten-week writing residency often described as the "United Nations of Writers." She is known locally as "Kuwait's Finest" slam poet. Her articles, poems, and/or fiction have been published in *The Norton Anthology of Hint Fiction, The New Left Project, Sukoon Magazine, Economic and Political Weekly, Divergent Voices, Kuwait Times, Arab Times*, and more.

SARAH GHOSHAL earned her MFA from Long Island University in Brooklyn and has two chapbooks, *Changing the Grid* (Finishing Line Press, 2015) and *The Pine Tree Experiment* (Lucky Bastard Press, 2015). Sarah recently received a Best of the Net nomination and her poetry can also be found in *Arsenic Lobster, Winter Tangerine Review, Reunion: The Dallas Review, Cream City Review* and *Red Savina Review*, among others. She lives in New Jersey with her husband, her happy little baby and their faithful dog, Comet, who flies through the air with the greatest of ease.

ALLISON JOSEPH is the author of several collections of poems, most recently *My Father's Kites* (Steel Toe Books), *Trace Particles* (Backbone Press), and *Little Epiphanies* (Imaginary Friend Press). She lives in Carbondale, Illinois, where she's on the faculty at Southern Illinois University.

DUSTIN KEATE is a recovering perpetual freshman and a US Army Power Plant Supervisor from Midland, TX. He currently lives in Fayetteville, NC. This is his first publication.

ATHENA KILDEGAARD is the author of three books of poetry; a fourth will appear early in 2016 from the new Tinderbox Editions. Recently her poems have appeared in *Grist, Zone 3, Barn Owl Review, Tinderbox Poetry Journal, Drunken Boat,* and *Up the Staircase Quarterly.*

CINDY KING lives in Lancaster, Texas, where she teaches at the University of North Texas Dallas as an Assistant Professor of English. In 2014, she was awarded a Tennessee Williams Scholarship to attend the Sewanee Writers' Workshop. Her most recent publications include poems in *Callaloo, North American Review, African American Review, American Literary Review, jubilat, River Styx, Barrow Street, The Pinch,* and elsewhere.

DANIELLE LAVAQUE-MANTY's short stories and flash fiction have appeared in *Glimmer Train, The Pinch, Monkeybicycle,* and *Midwestern Gothic.*

KEITH LESMEISTER lives and works in northeast Iowa. He holds an MFA from the Bennington Writing Seminars. His stories have appeared in *American Short Fiction, Meridian, Redivider, Harpur Palate, Columbia Review, Flyway,* and many others, with work forthcoming in *Gettysburg Review, Slice Magazine,* and *december.*

FABIYAS M V is a writer from Orumanayur village in Kerala, India. He is the author of *Moonlight* and *Solitude.* His fiction and poems have appeared in *Westerly, Forward Poetry, Literary The Hatchet, E Fiction, Off the Coast, Structo, Romantic Morsels,* and in several anthologies. He has won many international accolades, including the Poetry Soup International Award (USA), the RSPCA Pet Poetry Prize (UK), Speaking of Women Story Prize (Canada), and The Most Loved Poet For March 2014 Award by *E Fiction* (India). His poems have been broadcast on the All India Radio.

CARRIE MEADOWS' poetry has appeared in *North American Review, Mid-American Review, Dislocate, Prairie Schooner,* and other publications. She is a Hambidge fellow, a finalist for the Coniston Prize, and a finalist for the *Prairie Schooner* Book Prize in Poetry.

CATHERINE MOORE's writing has appeared in *Tahoma Literary Review, Southeast Review, Silver Birch Press, Southampton Review*, and in anthologies, most recently by Pankhearst Press. Her work garnered the 2014 Gearhart Poetry Prize and has been selected for inclusion in *The Best Small Fiction of 2015*. Her chapbook *Story* is available with Finishing Line Press. Catherine has a MFA from the University of Tampa. She is tweetable @CatPoetic.

GENEVIEVE PAYNE lives in Lewiston, Maine where she works as a team assistant for a non-profit health care agency. Her work has previously appeared in *Stolen Island* and *Scissors and Spackle*. She has work forthcoming in *Chagrin River Review*.

KATY PRZYBYLSKI is a student at Washington University in St. Louis studying English with a creative writing focus. This is her first print publication.

JAMES REED's work has appeared in such journals as *River Styx, The Gettysburg Review*, and *Quick Fiction*, and, among other awards, he holds an Individual Artist Fellowship from the Nebraska Arts Council.

AUTUMN RINALDI has been a contributing writer for Onstl.com for two years as a theatre reviewer and arts commentator. She is involved with the St. Louis Writers Guild and the (Un)Stable Writers Group. Some of her publications include "Left," which was featured in *Bareback Literary Magazine*, "The Night Before," in *The Rusty Nail*, and "The Shadow" in *The Weekenders Journal*.

JENN STROUD ROSSMANN is a professor of mechanical engineering at Lafayette College. Her stories have appeared most recently in *Night Train, Tahoma Literary Review, Dislocate*, and failbetter.com. She is a four-time Pushcart nominee. She has attended the *One Story, Tin House*, and Squaw Valley workshops.

SHANE STRICKER is originally from Sikeston, Missouri, though he completed his MFA at West Virginia University. He is currently in Morgantown teaching writing. His work appears in *Midwestern*

Gothic, Whitefish Review, Lake Effect, Crossborder, and Moon City Review.

M. K. SUKACH is the author of the chapbook, Something Impossible Happens (Big Wonderful Press), 2014. His poetry and reviews appear in a number of journals, including BlazeVox, Sharkpack Poetry Review, The Journal, Connotation Press, Spoon River Poetry Review, Construction Magazine, Yemassee, and others. www.mksukach.com.

ELLEN DAVIS SULLIVAN has had stories published in 94 Creations, Moment Magazine, and online in Catch & Release. Her essay, "The Perfect Height for Kissing," won the 2014 Columbia Nonfiction Prize and appears in Volume 53 of Columbia: A Journal of Literature and Art. She is a member of the Dramatists' Guild and her one-act plays have been produced around the country.

AMY JO SWING won a Loft Award in Poetry and a McKnight Foundation fellowship in 1998, as well as a Norcroft writing retreat residency in 2005. She's been published in journals such as The Laurel Review and Freefall, as well as poems included in two anthologies by Holy Cow! Press.

ELIJAH TUBBS is poetry editor for Superstition Review and a student at Arizona State University. He is founder of the forthcoming literary journal, ELKE.

the

IOWA REVIEW

iowareview.org
April, August, December
$20/year

TIR

People are just out there
struggling to make sense of life.
You have to give them something
they can use. It's only polite to do that.
—Anne Carson, Vol. 27.2

HE thousand injuries of Fortunato I had borne as I best could; but when he ventured upon insult, I vowed revenge. You, who so well know the nature of my soul, will not suppose, however, that I gave utterance to a threat. At length I would be avenged; this was a point definitively settled— but the very definitiveness with which it was resolved, precluded the idea of risk. I must not only punish, but punish with impunity. A wrong is unredressed when retribution overtakes its redresser. It is equally unredressed when the avenger fails to make himself felt as such to him who has done the wrong. It must be understood that neither by word nor dee   his face, and he did not perceiv   to—although in other regards h   e. Few Italians have the true vi   practise impos-ture upon the B   quack—but in

the matter of ol   Italian vintages myself, and bo   of the carnival season, that I e   The man wore motley. He had   was so pleased to see him, that   are luckily met.

How remarkably well you are looking to-day! But I have received a pipe of what passes for Amontillado, and I have my doubts."
"How?" said he. "Amontillado? A   ny doubts," I replied; "and I was silly enough to pay the full Amo   ot to be found, and I was fearful of losing a bargain." "Amontillac   em." "Amontillado!" "As you are engaged, I am on my way to Luc   "Luchesi cannot tell Amontillado from Sherry." "And yet some foc   , let us go." "Whither?" "To your vaults." "My friend, no; I will not   ement. Luchesi——" "I have no engagement;—come." "My frien   I perceive you are afflicted. The vaults are insufferably damp. Th   d is merely nothing. Amontillado! You have been imposed upon. A   lado." Thus speaking, Fortunato possessed himself of my arm. F   ely about my person, I suffered him to hurry me to my palazzo.   ake merry in honor of the time. I had told them that I should not   ot to stir from the house. These orders were sufficient, I well kne   on as my back was turned. I took from their sconces two flambeau   tes of rooms to the archway that led into the vaults. I passed dov   us as he followed. We came at length to the foot of the descent   f the Montresors. The gait of my friend was unsteady, and the be   s farther on," said I; "but observe the white webwork which gleam   into my eyes with two filmy orbs that distilled the rheum of intoxi   ong have you had that cough?" "Ugh! ugh! ugh!—ugh! ugh!   riend found it impossible to reply for many minutes. "It is nothing,   ck; your health is precious. You are rich, respected, admired, be   ssed. For me it is no matter. We will go back; you will be ill, and I   h," he said; "the cough is a mere nothing; it will not kill me. I shal   iad no intention of alarming you unnecessarily; but you should u   om the damps." Here I knocked off the neck of a bottle which I c   )rink," I said, presenting him the wine. He raised it to his lips with   jingled. "I drink," he said, "to the buried that repose around us." "A   ed. "These vaults," he said, "are extensive." "The Montresors," I r   s." "A huge human foot d'or, in a field azure; the foot crushes a s   l the motto?" "Nemo me impune lacessit." "Good!" he said. The v   grew warm with the Medoc. We had passed through walls of pile   nost recesses of the catacombs. I paused again, and this time I n   e nitre!" I said; "see, it increases. It hangs like moss upon the vau   le among the bones. Come, we will go back ere it is too late. Yo   another draught of the Medoc." I broke and reached him a flagor   h a fierce light. He laughed and threw the bottle upward with a g   He repeated the movement—a grotesque one. "You do not con   e brotherhood." "How?" "You are not of the masons." "Yes, yes," I   lied. "A sign," he said. "It is this," I answered, producing a trowel   ned, recoiling a few paces. "But let us proceed to the Amontillad   t again offering him my arm. He leaned upon it heavily. We cont   ough a range of low arches, de-scended, passed on, and desc   f the air caused our flambeaux rather to glow than flame. At the most remote end of the crypt there appeared another less spacious. Its walls had been lined with human remain   f this interior crypt were still ornamen   sly upon the earth, forming at one po   e perceived a still interior recess, in   icted for no espe-cial use within itse   lacombs, and was backed by one of   ch, endeavored to pry into the depth   erein is the Amon-tillado. As for Luc   I, while I followed immediately at his   ested by the rock, stood stupidly bev   on staples, distant from each other a   adlock. Throwing the links about his   esist. Withdrawing

the key I stepped back from the recess. "Pass your hand," I said, "over the wall; you cannot help feeling the nitre. Indeed it is very damp. Once more let me implore you to return. No? Then I must positively leave you. But I must first render you all the little attentions in my power." "The Amontillado!" ejaculated my friend, not yet recovered from his astonishment. "True," I re-plied; "the Amontillado." As I said these words I busied myself among the pile of bones of which I have before spoken. Throw-

www.ingramcontent.com/pod-product-compliance
Lightning Source LLC
Chambersburg PA
CBHW061243170626
46809CB00007B/2811